THE ENGLISH THEATRE

THE ROMAN THEATRE, VERULAMIUM (ST. ALBANS).

THE
ENGLISH THEATRE

A SHORT HISTORY

by

ALLARDYCE NICOLL

GREENWOOD PRESS, PUBLISHERS
WESTPORT, CONNECTICUT

The Library of Congress cataloged this book as follows:

Nicoll, Allardyce, 1894–
    The English theatre; a short history. Westport, Conn.,
Greenwood Press ₁1970₎

    xi, 252 p. illus. 23 cm.

    Reprint of the 1936 ed.
    Based on the author's The English stage.
    Bibliography: p. 229–233.

    1. Theater—London—History. 2. Theater—England—History.
I. Title.

PN2581.N5   1970   792′.09421   75–98861
ISBN 0–8371–3133–2   MARC

   Library of Congress   71 ₁7₎

Originally published in 1936 by Thomas Nelson and Sons,
Ltd., London

Reprinted in 1970 by Greenwood Press, Inc.,
51 Riverside Avenue, Westport, CT 06880

Library of Congress catalog card number 75-98861
ISBN 0-8371-3133-2

Printed in the United States of America

10 9 8 7 6 5 4 3 2

PREFACE

JULIUS CÆSAR is dead ; Mr. James Smith is living and breathing in our midst. The one we meet and say we know, the other we can only know of through such scattered facts as time has preserved for us. To affirm, however, because the one lives and the other is but dust, that only the former deserves our attention were manifestly absurd. Dry and fragmentary though the evidence may be, a vital image of the long-vanished Cæsar may be born in our minds, clearer and more arresting than the actual picture of Mr. James Smith as he passes across our view.

The theatre of Shakespeare, of Congreve, of Sheridan, the theatre in which Burbage and Betterton and Garrick performed, may be, like Julius Cæsar, dead, but there is a value in re-constructing its vanished forms akin to that achieved in recapturing the personalities who have affected the course of history. True, the stage presents an art-form essentially impermanent. Only for a brief two hours' traffic on the boards does a performance endure, and an actor's skill dies as soon as born. Of that which went to make up a production all that will remain is the bare text of the play, a few scene designer's sketches at the most, some managerial notes, two or three

scattered records set down by eye-witnesses before
or behind the curtain. At first sight it seems
impossible to recapture the thrill and wonder with
which the original audiences were invested; profit-
less to attempt any examination of these lifeless
relics which alone remain, like the shattered form
of Ozymandias, to tell of tragic amazement and
of comedy's merriment. No more difficult, however, is this effort than that of shaping forth in
vital form the lives of men now gone to their
graves. Out of a thousand separate facts, each
one in itself valueless or unintelligible, may be
built a vivid biography ; and similarly may be
created an imaginative reconstruction of Elizabethan Globe or eighteenth-century Drury Lane,
which, while perhaps wanting in some details,
presents all the essentials necessary for a keen
relishing of Shakespeare's power or of Garrick's
variegated skill.

To achieve this end, obviously a great deal
must be done in the amassing of such evidence
as may serve our purposes, and, in spite of the
fact that there is already existent a fairly extensive
theatrical library, much remains for students to
assemble, classify, and annotate. Until this material is fully gathered the complete picture
cannot be created, any more than an adequate
biography can be formulated out of barely half
the available facts. Towards the ultimate goal
we have moved far during the past hundred
years, but even the efforts of this century have
not placed before us all we should wish to know.

In this volume, covering in short space the
fortunes of the stage from the beginnings to the
present day, no attempt, naturally, has been made
to add to this existing store of knowledge. The
presentation of fact, indeed, has here been reduced to a minimum, since to bring forward
fresh documentary evidence would have been
likely to overbalance an account which aims solely
at providing a rapid survey of traditions, of
changing forms, and of ideals succeeding ideals.

For the same reason I have presented such
original material as seemed necessary in a form
likely not to puzzle the general reader ; normally
where the texts quoted offered no serious difficulties in interpretation these are presented un-
altered, but I have not hesitated on occasion to
modernize either in whole or in part. To give
a general accompaniment to the reading of
drama has been my aim. I shall consider my
task accomplished if I have added in any way to
the appreciative reading of the dramatic texts
available to us, and if, from a perusal of these
pages, a few students at least are encouraged to
apply themselves to the building up of that body of
information which will give us the foundation for
a clearer and more comprehensive understanding
of what the theatre has meant to our forefathers.

This volume takes the place of a smaller book
(*The English Stage*) published several years ago.
While based on the latter, *The English Theatre* has
been entirely rewritten, and covers a much more
extended field than was possible in the limited

scope of the earlier essay. Perhaps, in making this statement, I should also draw attention to the fact that *The English Theatre*, devoted mainly to the history of the stage in London, does not in any way profess to cover the ground surveyed in *The Development of the Theatre*. That work is concerned with the playhouse in all lands; it deals with a much larger territory, and consequently includes material on the English stage only in its relation to the stage as a whole. While some aspects of the subject are there more fully treated, others, such as the changing styles in histrionic interpretation, find no place. The two volumes are therefore complementary.

To the Right Honourable the Earl of Cromer I wish to express my thanks for permission to peruse and abstract information from the register of theatre licences at St. James's Palace; some of this information is incorporated in the list of London playhouses printed as an appendix to this volume. At the same time I desire to acknowledge my indebtedness to the authorities of the Victoria and Albert Museum, from whose co-operation and assistance I have benefited on this occasion as on many occasions in the past. Mr. John Hampden, General Editor of Thomas Nelson and Sons, has aided me both by the preparation of the index to this volume and by his friendly co-operation in bringing my pages to the press.

Yale University   A. N.

CONTENTS

ILLUSTRATIONS

THE ENGLISH THEATRE

CHAPTER I

MEDIÆVAL

RECENT excavations have brought to light a spacious amphitheatre at Caerleon, and at Verulamium, the modern St. Albans, a well-proportioned Roman playhouse. These two relics of the third century testify to the existence among the early Britons of such forms of entertainment as delighted the citizens of the imperial city itself. Here, with these relics, we stand at the beginnings of the English stage.

That England at this period produced nothing characteristic, that it merely shared in whatever was in vogue throughout the entire scope of the Empire, is certain, but we can hardly believe that the traditions established by that theatre at Verulamium and by that amphitheatre at Caerleon were completely forgotten during the centuries that followed the departure of the legions about the year 400. In England, as elsewhere in Europe, the modern drama did not arise until in the tenth century the clergy organized performances in association with the regular services of the Catholic Church. Far removed these seem

from the tragedies and comedies known to a
Pericles and a Cæsar ; yet to understand aright
the way in which this mediæval religious theatre
came into being, and to assess correctly the forms
of entertainment developed during succeeding
centuries, we must first glance at and endeavour
to appreciate those theatrical conventions which,
established in classical Greece and carried thence to
imperial Rome, exercised an influence both direct
and indirect upon the slowly evolving playhouses
and stages of other lands and of other times.

During the classical period two distinct types
of staging were familiar—the well-known " classical " stage, with a long narrow platform backed
by a scene-building in which were three or five
doors of entrance, and the more elusive " popular "
stage, of wooden boards and trestles, set up as
occasion demanded either by amateurs among
distant Dorian villages or by later professionals
in diverse parts of the Roman Empire. For the
former were penned the tragedies of Æschylus,
Sophocles, Euripides, and the comedies of Aris-
tophanes; on the latter were performed rude
satirical farces, hardly owning any formal authors,
and the mimes, or improvised playlets, which, by
the third century, had come to oust the literary
productions of Terence and Plautus from the
boards. The poetic tragedy and comedy usually
were closely confined both in the fictional time
of their action and in the localities supposed to
form their settings ; but to restrict the period
of plot development to the actual time occupied

by the performance or to keep the setting to one single place was found either disadvantageous or impossible. Hence even in the simplicity of this classical theatre the necessity arose for finding some means of presenting several different localities in the course of a single play. A solution was discovered, first, in providing the doors of entrance with symbolic associations (so that the central doorway might be taken as representing the portals of a palace, that on the right the way to a temple and that on the left the entrance to a prison), and, later, in indicating these localities by means of painted boards (*pinakes*), the beginnings of modern stage design. As will be obvious, while in general there was a striving for a "unity of place," this system frequently introduced at one time two or three localities which, in reality, would have been far separated from each other. Just as the dramatists found necessary a kind of foreshortening of time whereby many more episodes were crushed into an hour's length than that hour could possibly have included, so they devised for themselves a foreshortening in space. Thus was the multiple or simultaneous set, usually considered the product of the Middle Ages, brought into being.

On the more primitive stages of the amateur farce-players and the mimes such a solution could not serve, for there no scene-building provided a background to the actors : at most these performers would have a piece of cloth stretched on a thin frame (the Roman *siparium*) against which they might present their shows. For them, clearly, but one method was open—the imaginative creation of *local* by word and action. This meant that to them dramatic space was unlimited; their platform might become whatever they wished to make it. Now it could represent a courtyard in front of a palace, now a temple, now the heights of Parnassus; nothing restricted them, because everything lay in the world of fancy and a sentence was sufficient to change the scene from exterior to interior, from city square to haunt of the gods.

Both these principles in staging were carried on to the close of the Roman Empire. True, the production of literary plays rapidly ceded place to the more vigorous gambolling of the mimes, but knowledge at least of the more formal methods endured even while the trestle-stage of the professional entertainers was more familiar to experience. Then came the inrushing hordes of barbarians from the north and the east. The firmly built-up frontiers of the Empire shook and finally crumbled; back the legions were summoned to defend Rome itself, and even their massed ranks failed to stem the roaring tide of flushed savage faces that poured over the Alps, destroying as it went the glories of an ancient culture. In the torrent the theatres were submerged, not wholly destroyed but, their use no longer remembered, left to crumble in decay. This, however, does not imply that the practice of playing likewise perished. Professional actors still plied their trade throughout the lands which once had been

Rome's. Generations of barbarian rule succeeding one another, no doubt these actors lost in the turmoil much of their old repertory and, confronted alike by rising religious prejudice and by uncultured indifference, their productions must soon have degenerated in content and in scope; but, whatever loss and whatever decadence, they still preserved intact something at least of that which had been seen by a Marcus Aurelius and a Seneca. They became the ancestors of the jongleurs who made merry many a mediæval mansion and many a lonely village throughout the length and breadth of Europe in days that were dark.

How precisely a new drama arose in the tenth century we may only guess. That such a drama developed out of the services of the Church is unquestioned, but it seems probable that this development came, partly at least, from the endeavours on the part of ecclesiastical authorities to battle with the profane force of the jongleurs and the equally profane force of those May games and village mummings, the true antiquity of which can never be told, performed in a thousand townships and hamlets from prehistoric times down even to our own days. From a liturgical beginning with simple chanted dialogue, this new drama developed until it assumed the vast proportions of the mystery cycle; sometimes, as in those scenes where Mrs. Noah plays the shrew with her husband or where a thievish Mak steals one of the flock of his fellow-shepherds, it embraced within its reach the merriment of the secular entertainers, and those secular entertainers themselves continued, despised by authority and adored by the folk, to perform their rude farces in which a licentious lover seeks the aid of an old witch in his pursuit of a cruel maiden, or a rascally priest makes fun of the husband whose wife he has taken for himself.

These mediæval plays—early liturgical dramas in Latin or in the vernacular, as yet an integral part of the services of the Church, mystery cycles which showed the entire history of the world as presented in the Bible, miracles of the saints derived from the *Acta Sanctorum* or from popular legend, and secular farces often of a licentious kind—were not produced on one single type of stage, but all the separate stages agreed in bowing to one set of conventions. It all starts with the performances of the *mimi*, or *jongleurs*, and with the more solemn productions within the mediæval Church. If we imagine to ourselves a couple of vagrant entertainers of the Middle Ages preparing themselves to delight an audience, we realize that the " setting " for their dialogue will have to be of the slightest. Perhaps a cart in a market square or a dais in a hall represents the utmost in the way of staging they could secure. Perhaps—if, for example, they pretend that they are in a tavern—a table and benches may be used to give a semblance of that locality, but in the main the localization of the stage must depend upon their own words and actions. Still further, when a change of " scene " is required, the different actors—or the same actors

in different rôles—must, by their very presence,
alter the fictional locality of the cart or the dais.
The method, indeed, was exactly that employed
by the Roman *mimi*; so that the performers of
secular farces in mediæval times were but adopting
the scenic devices used by their ancestors many
centuries previous.

This type of setting is carried directly over to
the religious theatre. The religious theatre starts
in the Church itself. During the Easter ceremonials, priests, arrayed in white, seat themselves
by the altar or in front of the crypt stairs; three
other priests, also arrayed in white and simulating
three women, wander anxiously down the nave.
The first greets them :

" *Quem quæritis in sepulchro, [o] Christicolæ?*
(Whom do you seek in the sepulchre, O
Christian women ?) "

he inquires, and they, looking up, answer him :

" *Iesum Nazarenum crucifixum, o cœlicolæ !*
(Jesus of Nazareth who was crucified, O
Heavenly Ones !) "

Then the first priest makes reply :

" *Non est hic, surrexit sicut prædixerat.*
Ite, nuntiate quia surrexit de sepulchro.
(He is not here ; He has risen even as he
predicted.
Go, announce that He has arisen from the
dead.) "

And the choir, in joyous strain, chant out the glad tidings. The drama is done. Now, here, in primitive form, we have all the essentials of a theatrical performance. The words of the angel indicate both the locality and the nature of those who come to Him, while the words of the three Maries in turn show the character of their questioner. " Whom do you seek ? " and " Jesus of Nazareth " by themselves would not have formed genuine dramatic dialogue ; the words as presented in this tenth-century *Quem quæritis* playlet do. Here, however, matters are simple, for only one locality is shown. More complicated become the early Christmas plays where we see, first the birth of Christ, then the announcement to the shepherds, and lastly the wanderings of the three kings. In presenting such a series, two methods seem to have been adopted by the ecclesiastical " producers " of the plays.

The first was merely an extension of the " open stage " or unlocalized stage of the secular players. In the scene of the three kings, for example, it would be sufficient to have three priests moving from different parts of the church and meeting in some free space, which, from their words, would become (temporarily, during their staying there) a field outside of Bethlehem. When these actors crossed over to Joseph and Mary, that portion of the church which but a moment before had been thus localized would become nothing but ordinary church again. More commonly, however, some attempt was made in the visual suggestion of a place of action. The sepulchre of Christ became either a special structure built for the occasion or else something introduced architecturally into the church building, and once this sepulchre had so been realized in actuality it was but natural that other locations should similarly be delineated. In the Easter play a stall set up for the unguent-seller established one such position ; at Christmas others would be apportioned to the shepherds, to Bethlehem, and so on, in accordance with the demands of the script. Strangely akin to the principles involved in classical staging, this gradually developing simultaneous setting, wherein many places were shown at one time to the audience, seems to have come untaught to the ecclesiastics who sponsored these early mediæval shows, and untaught it grew until, for the more elaborate productions of the kind, the entire floor of the cathedral nave and choir was dotted with such locations, variously named as " mansions," " houses," " sedes," or " estals," because originally they marked the " seat " or " house " of this character or of that, representing everything from cities (such as Jerusalem) to the dwellings of individuals (such as the " mansion " of Herod).

To this extended form did the mediæval religious play grow within the confines of cathedral walls, but, growing, it gradually drew upon itself the suspicion of the ecclesiastical authorities. At the beginning the religious drama had been merely an extension of the liturgy, of the Church services ;

but now these elaborate productions, especially
when they cast over the Church Latin in favour
of a more easily understood vernacular, could not
pretend to be aught save independent shows, and,
while it was recognized that the original impetus
had been purely a religious one, two potential
sources of danger were discovered.

In the first place, this novelty appealed to the
people for its own sake. The enacting of liturgical
plays tended to cast a shadow over the other
services of the Church. And, secondly, the introduction of the vernacular was proving perilous.
How soon this intruded we do not know ; but
we are aware of the fact that, even before the
childlike drama had left the bounds of the Church,
English and French and German words were
occasionally to be heard amidst the sonorous
Latin. Fearing these things, the authorities tried
to stifle that to which they themselves had given
birth ; but the drama had come to stay, and,
when attempts were made to suppress it in the
church, it merely ran outside to the churchyard,
and soon established itself, in a purely vernacular
form, in the market square or on the village green.
Rapidly it grew, until from that four-lined *Quem
quæritis* origin, it developed into the vast cycles
of mystery plays with their tens of thousands of
verses. Naturally, this fuller dramatic development had to be accompanied by a fuller development theatrically ; but always there clung to
these performances the initial impress of the
liturgical setting.

The normal mediæval mystery " theatre " consisted of an auditorium which was nothing more
than a village green, a street corner, or a market
square. Occasionally a special structure might be
used, as when, in Southern France, ancient Roman
amphitheatres were employed, or when, in the far
west of Cornwall, special rounds of earth or stone
were built by village communities for their plays.
The usual auditorium, however, either provided
no seating accommodation for the audience, or,
at the most, boasted a few raised benches for
specially privileged spectators. The stage itself
seems to have taken a variety of different forms,
all dependent upon one common idea. This
common idea was the presentation of a piece of
unlocalized ground with the accompaniment of
several localized positions—a combination of the
simultaneous setting and the bare platform used
by the Roman *mimi* and by later itinerant entertainers. The unlocalized space was known technically as the *platea*, anglicized as " place " or (in
Cornwall) as " plain." This " place," forming
the main " stage " and roughly corresponding to
the acting ground in the cathedral nave, might be
merely the street itself, the village green, the centre
of the round amphitheatrical structure ; on the
other hand, it might be, and often was, a raised
platform, bare of properties or of scenic adornment.
Like the floor of the church in the days of liturgical
drama, it formed a general acting-ground which
could be " anywhere," changing its imaginative
significance with the succession of different

characters. In addition to the *platea*, we find the "mansions," simple pieces of symbolic setting which indicated definite localities. These mansions, as has been seen, already were known when the theatre was still the church, but naturally, once the drama had moved from within the ecclesiastical buildings to the free and unsanctified out-of-doors, changes came in the general arrangement of these primitive pieces of scenery. In general, two main methods are to be traced. The first of these is the "standing scene," wherein the mansions were placed together along a straight wall, or semicircularly, or in an amphitheatre, or according to the ideal plan of a mediæval church. Thus, for one performance anything from half a dozen to thirty or forty mansions might be set alongside each other, representing localities as far distant as Heaven and Hell, Jerusalem and Rome. The *platea* in front would indicate at one time the land between Jerusalem and Rome, the space between Heaven and Hell, and at another would be temporarily localized by a group of actors who found that they had to represent a place unprovided for in any mansion. Usually in these "standing scenes" the various mansions were arranged according to a strict orientation. The East traditionally was the place of Heaven or Paradise, and, since the Bible itself had declared that "evil appeareth out of the North," Hell was often placed in that direction. Some confusion, however, tended to enter in because of the desire to put Hell as far away from Heaven as possible. In

the two most famous miniatures depicting the
multiple settings of mystery plays (the Valen-
ciennes miniature and that by Jehan Fouquet
showing the martyrdom of St. Apollonia), Heaven
is set to the left of the spectator, with Hell at the
extreme right, and this seems to have been their
most common positions. In between the two
extremes the other mansions found their appropriate sites.

Not always, however, were the mansions arranged as a " standing scene." Occasionally on
the Continent, and regularly in England, this
standing scene was split up, the separate mansions,
now called " pageants," were placed on wheels,
and the whole mystery cycle was produced in a
series of concurrent performances, the birth of
Christ being shown at the same time as, at another
street corner, the massacre of the innocents was
being enacted. Descriptions of these pageants
have come down to us. Apparently they consisted
of a two-floored " stage," the lower floor being
curtained all round to form a dressing-room—
" a highe place made like a howse with 2
rowmes [rooms], being open on ye tope ; [in] the
lower rowme they apparrelled and dressed themselves ; and in the higher rowme they played."
The scenic action thus took place on the upper
floor, and possibly a ladder or steps permitted
the performers to descend to the street level.
" Here Erode [Herod] ragis in the pagond [pag-
eant] and in the strete also " is a stage direction
from one of these plays, which indicates how

the actors moved freely from one position to the other.

The mansions and the pageants must have presented scenic decoration largely of a symbolic character. In the very early Anglo-Norman play of *Adam*, written by one Hilarius, we are told of the flowers which adorned Paradise, and flowers seem also to have flourished in Heaven. " Let Paradyce be fynely made," runs a stage direction in a Cornish play, " wyth two fayre trees in yt and an appell upon the tree and som other frute one the other," with further admonitions to have there " a fowntaine and fyne flowers in yt painted." Hell belched forth its flames from the mouth of a hideous dragon's head and showed the torments of sinful souls in an adjoining chamber of horrors. At Coventry fourpence was paid a man " for keeping fyer at Hell's mouth," and in Cornwall at least there was some kind of theatrical mechanism which caused that Hell-mouth to " gape." For the play of *Noah's Ark* the pageant itself represented a ship, whilst the pageant for the drama of *Christ and the Doctors* seems to have been shaped in the form of a temple.

The gaping Hell-mouth of Cornwall makes us wonder how much of mechanical apparatus the English stage employed. That machinery proved a vastly popular element in France may readily be demonstrated ; the stage-manager's promptbook of the mystery play at Mons, discovered and edited by Gustave Cohen, is a formidable document and teems with instructions relating to

Reproduced from " The Development of the Theatre " (Harrap).

TWO MEDIÆVAL PAGEANTS.
From a MS. in the Bodleian Library, Oxford.

things of this kind. Hell-mouths that opened
and shut were the least of the marvels that French
audiences demanded ; for them the technical
" secrets " or " feyntes " provided a good proportion of the entertainment to be gained from
watching a show. One suspects that in England
things were more simply managed, although it
is true that several stage-directions demand contrivances of a mechanical sort. A glorious re-
volving sphere on occasion ornamented Heaven.
Angels freely descended and rose again. Christ
was borne to the top of the pinnacle by means
of a rope and pulley. Devils vanished through
trap-doors. Suddenly lights flashed in a splendour.
If we were to accept the directions literally, we
should be compelled to believe that there were
machines for creating earthquakes and others for
setting " the world on fire." Even, however, if
the earthquake was only a falling pillar and the
flaming world but a toy, we must recognize that
at least a certain amount of purely theatrical
ingenuity was applied to the production of the
plays. Interpretation was not kept simple and
ritualistically pure : the crackling of squibs and
the creaking of ropes accompanied the enunciation
of God's blessing and the last agonized cry of
Jesus. " Let them fight with swordis," runs a
stage-direction in a Cornish play, " and in the
end Lucyfer voydeth [departs] and goeth downe
to hell apareled fowle with fyre about hem turn-
ing to hell and every degre of devylls of lether and
spirytis on cordis runing into ye playne and so

remayne there nine angells after Lucyfer goeth
to hell." In England as in France these devices
must have pleased the spectators, and at times no
doubt have given anxiety to the performers. At
Seurre in 1496

> he who took the part of Satan, as he was about
> to ascend from his below-stage trap, had his
> clothes catch fire so that he got badly burned ;
> but he was speedily dragged out, stripped and
> reclothed, and so was enabled, without any
> show of disturbance, to proceed with his role.

The dangers of Hell were dangers indeed.
" Apparelled foul " were the devils ; and the
note reminds us that some considerable endeavour
was made to secure variety of costuming. Presumably many of the characters appeared in garments of the day—such in fact are alluded to
even in the texts of mystery plays—and ecclesiastical raiment was freely used for the Deity, for
priests, and perhaps even for kings. At the same
time numbers of the persons introduced into the
plays must have been granted special costumes.
The leather suits for the devils were everywhere
familiar ; and such a type as Herod seems to have
worn clothes befitting his character. Sometimes
he had a mask (called " head " or " face "), for
adorning which painters were paid fourpence a
time, his richly ornamented gown cost at Coventry
thirteen shillings and sevenpence, and three new
plates in his iron crest were credited for another

fourpence. Furred gowns were apportioned to
the doctors, and angels sported their traditional
wings. Alongside of these would appear Herod's
courtier in gallant caparison, and Mary Magdalen,
in her *mondanité*, dressed according to the latest
fashions of the time.

The admixture of costumes corresponds to the
general principles of staging employed. Conventional symbolism, well-known and appreciated
through the art of the Church, combined with
efforts of an almost childish nature in the direction
of realism. In details, if not in larger effects,
audiences of the period demanded much. Should
there occur a scene of massacre, then blood in
bladders was imperatively called for. A few
painted trees might serve for the garden of Eden,
but when God had to create Eve then " a rib
coloured red " had always to be ready for His
hand. The spectators could readily imagine a
simple platform into the city of Jerusalem, but
they were unable to do without the ordinary things
of real life.

A similar blending of the conventional and
the naturalistic seems to have characterized the
methods of interpretation employed by the actors.
These actors, be it remembered, after the first
period when the new drama was but a part of
the liturgy, were chiefly members of the town
guilds, assisted, perhaps, at times by professional
entertainers. Only by amateurs could the long
series of mystery plays have been produced,
demanding as they did a host of major and minor

figures. It was the town guild which, by a tax
on its incorporates, financed the preparation of
the plays, the copying of the parts, the building
of the pageants, the costuming of the characters.
Very solemnly and with a due sense of importance
did men set about this work. In 1476 the York
town council decreed

> that yearly in the time of Lent there shall be
> called before the mayor for the time being four
> of the most cunning (skilful), discreet, and able
> players within this city, to search, hear, and
> examine all the players and plays and pageants
> throughout all the artificers belonging to [the]
> Corpus Christi play. And all such as they shall
> find sufficient in person and cunning (skill), to
> the honour of the city and worship of the said
> crafts, for to admit and able ; and all other
> insufficient persons, either in cunning, voice,
> or person to discharge, ammove (remove) and
> avoid (reject).

" Pageant-masters " were regularly appointed
officials ; and the text of the plays, called variously
the " original " or the " reginal," was a carefully
treasured document.

The solemnity and care, of course, must often
enough have been of a rather ludicrous sort, akin
to the seriousness with which Bottom and Quince
and Starveling set about the preparation of a play
for Theseus. In sixteenth-century France—and
the conditions were similar to those in England—

we hear that both actors and " producers " of
the mysteries

> are an ignorant set of men, mechanical artisans,
> knowing not an A or a B, untrained and un-
> skilled in playing such pieces before the public ;
> their voices are poor, their language unfitting,
> their pronunciation wretched ; no sense do
> they have of the meaning of what they say.
> Often enough they make three words out of one,
> and stop short in the middle of a sentence ; at
> a note of interrogation they make a gesture of
> wonder or the like, and give a tone and accent
> hopelessly at variance with their speeches.
> Hence often they are jeered at and hissed . . .
> so that their playing is turned from edification
> to a piece of folly.

This truly is in Bottom's vein :

If we offend, it is with our good will.
That you should thinke, we come not to offend,
But with good will.   To shew our simple skill,
That is the true beginning of our end.
Consider then, we come but in despight.
We do not come, as minding to content you,
Our true intent is.   All for your delight,
We are not heere.

Shakespeare was but revealing the mediæval
amateurs at a time when, caught by the spirit of
the Renaissance, they were beginning to abandon
their Biblical tales in favour of ancient legend.

" But, masters," says Quince, " here are your parts," and normally in mediæval times too the great " original " (what Quince is already calling the " scrip ") was so copied out for the use of the individual actors. Such at least seems to have been common practice for the acting of all the mystery dramas in English. For the Cornish plays, however, a different procedure was followed, for there the prompt book or " ordinale " was held in the hands of one man who read out the lines to the various actors. Of this method Carew has a word to say in his *Survey*. Referring to the " guary miracle (in English, a miracle play)," he observes that

for representing it, they raise an earthen amphi-theatre in some open field, having the diameter of its enclosed plain some 40 or 50 foot. The country people flock from all sides, many miles off, to hear and see it ; for they have therein devils and devices to delight as well the eye as the ear ; the players con not their parts without book, but are prompted by one called the ordinary, who followeth at their back with the book in his hand and telleth them softly what they must pronounce aloud, which manner once gave occasion to a pleasant conceited gentleman of practising a merry prank : for he undertaking (perhaps of set purpose) an actor's room, was accordingly lessoned before-hand by the ordinary, that he must say after him. His turn came : quoth the ordinary,

"Go forth, man, and shew thyself." The gentleman steps out upon the stage, and, like a bad clerk in scripture manners, cleaving more to the letter than the sense, pronounced those words aloud. "Oh" (says the fellow softly in his ear), "you mar all the play." And with this his passion, the actor makes the audience in like sort acquainted. Hereon the prompter falls to flat railing and cursing in the bitterest terms he could devise : which the gentleman with a set gesture and countenance still soberly related, until the ordinary, driven at last into a mad rage, was fain to give over all. Which trousse, though it brake off the interlude, yet defrauded not the beholders, but dismissed them with a great deal more sport and laughter, than 20 such guares could have afforded.

Whether the normal English or the Cornish method was employed, however, general conditions must have remained fundamentally akin. Of sincerity and vigour in the histrionic interpretation there must have been much, but of polished rendering and of technical skill virtually nothing. Without a doubt, the methods of acting must have changed as the plays were taken from within the church to the market square, but a great deal of the earlier traditions would certainly have been carried over to the new surroundings even while a greater naturalism, noisiness, and clamour began to intrude. When the mediæval drama was still part of the liturgy, the chanting

of the characters readily harmonized with the
familiar chanting of the Church services, and any
gestures introduced naturally approximated those
of a symbolic kind adopted by the priest before
the altar. Even at the very beginning, on the
other hand, at a time when dialogue was but
scanty and the dressing of the dramatic persons
hardly indicated clearly to the eyes what they were
intended to represent, much use is likely to have
been made of gesture which, although conventional,
might serve to make the action more intelligible.
An early French play instructs the actors that
when they mention Paradise they should point at
it, and this procedure, obviously eminently de-
sirable when the " mansion " but crudely indicated its scope, probably was followed largely in
all European countries.

In certain performances without a doubt mimic
gesture supplied the spectators' imaginations with
nearly all these required for a proper appreciation
of the sacred story unfolded before them, and we
may conceive of actors pretending things, in a
manner similar to that in which members of the
modern " Compagnie des Quinze " created out
of empty air the dove that brought back glad
tidings to Noah. Many mediæval stage-directions
suggest an " as if," the performer naturalistically
or symbolically creating what was lacking to
sight. On the other hand, such mimic action
frequently was dispensed with in favour of other
methods. Both in France and England evidence
is available which points to the use of painted

objects intended to appeal directly to the spectators' eyes. Typical of the two methods are
some directions in the Chester *Deluge*. First
" Noe with all his familye shall make a signe as
though the (they) wrought vpon the shippe with
divers instruements." Here the " as though "
suggests the pretence of action and not its presentation. Shortly after, however, " Noe shall
goe into the Arke with all his familye, his wyffe
excepte, and the arke must bee borded rownde
about, and one (on) the bordes all the beastes
and fowles here after rehersed muste bee paynted
that ther (their) wordes may agree with the pictures." In that instruction we recognize the
operation of another and opposed principle.

Of detailed evidence concerning histrionic
method, it is true, hardly more than a few scraps
of information have come down to us. Perhaps
the most interesting document is a *Processional*
belonging to fourteenth - century Cividale, the
stage-directions of which are exceptionally numerous. From them, maybe, a vague impression may
be gained of the way in which the Maries appeared
to contemporary audiences.

> *Magdalen. (Here she turns to the men with her
> arms extended)* O my brothers ! *(Here to the
> women)* O my sisters ! Where is my hope ?
> *(Here she beats her breast)* Where is my con-
> solation ? *(Here she raises her hands)* Where is
> my whole well-being ? *(Here, head inclined, she
> throws herself at Christ's feet)* O my Master !

Mary Major. (*Here she points to Mary Magdalen*) O Mary Magdalen, (*Here she points to
Christ*) sweet disciple of my son, (*Here she
embraces Magdalen, putting both her arms around
her neck*) weep with me, in grief, (*Here she
points to Christ*) over the death of my sweet
son (*Here she points to Magdalen*) and the death
of your master, (*Here she points to Christ*) the
death of him (*Here she points to Magdalen*) who
so loved you, (*Still pointing to Magdalen*) who
all your sins (*Here she lets her arms fall*) has
taken from you. (*Here she embraces Magdalen,
as before, while she says*) Most sweet Magdalen.

Magdalen. (*Here she greets Mary with her
hands*) Mother of Jesus crucified, (*Here she
weeps*) with you do I weep over the death of
Christ.

Mary, Mother of James. (*Here she makes a
wide gesture over the audience and then puts her
hands before her eyes*) Who is there here who
would not weep, seeing the mother of Christ
(*Here she beats her breast*) in such misery ?

These directions seem to leave no room for
doubt that the characteristic method was one in
which every endeavour was made to reveal clearly,
by precise gesture and indication, what might be
misinterpreted or remain unintelligible. When
the Virgin weeps she is bidden to express her grief
through her gestures as well as through her tears ;
she is told to open wide her arms and sink to the

ground ; her words have to come from her in a
" tearful voice." At the same time, we must
remember that, if there was this searching for
interpretative action of a symbolic or realistically
appropriate kind, contemporary taste called for a
restraint harmonizing at once with the solemn
subject-matter of the plays and with the priestly
gestures employed in the services of the Church.
" The Blessed Virgin," runs a rubric in a Latin
text of German origin, " now extends her arms
widely and now raises her hands as she gazes at
her son—but all in moderation." Conventional
movements satisfied the spectators, and Cohen is
amply justified in his remark that the actors presented to the public a series of movements " which
seemed to them necessarily those of God or his
angels," and did not try to " reproduce the
gestures of daily life." The aim was to make the
ideal images formed of sacred characters take
shape in visible form. Unquestionably methods
must have become bolder and stronger when the
cycles of mystery plays developed in the hands of
the amateur actors belonging to the town guilds,
but even in the latest religious theatre of the
sixteenth century a certain " moderation in gesture " was demanded.

Comic elements, however, soon began to intrude into the themes of religious devotion, and
in such comic scenes little of this symbolic
gesturing can have been introduced. Rather must
the interpretation have borrowed from the ruder
and more boisterous methods of the secular

entertainers.   Lucifer and his devils, soon transformed into partly if not wholly ludicrous persons,
roared and tumbled, while Herod was made
ridiculous by his bombastic " raging."   Mak and
his shepherds, in their amusing interlude preceding the appearance of the star, can have performed in no wise save as rude peasants, dull-
witted and unrefined of speech, lazily watching
their flocks.

One suspects, indeed, that two sharply marked
styles appeared in the acting of these mystery
plays, corresponding to the two styles in their
composition.   On the one hand, there was the
serious Biblical material, solemn in its import and
closely to be allied to the liturgical ceremonials
within the church, and, on the other, the intrusive
matter of invented sort, rich with comic vigour
and bearing a definite relationship to the farcical
entertainments of wandering professional actors.
Both must have found their " cunning, discreet,
and able " interpreters ; and we can well imagine
what excitement prevailed in lonely mediæval
communities as the time approached for try-outs
and rehearsals, the latter freely interspersed with
refreshments in the form of beef and ale.   And an
equal excitement must have been occasioned when
the messenger rode round the town crying his
proclamation or " banns " :

Oyez, oyez, oyez. We command of the King's
behalf and the Mayor and the sheriffs of this
city that no man go armed in this city with

swords nor with Carlill-axes, nor none other
defences in disturbance of the King's peace and
the play, or hindering of the procession of
Corpus Christi, and that they leave their
harness in their inns, saving knights and
squires of worship that owe (have the right
to) have swords borne after them, of (on) pain
of forfeiture of their weapons and imprisonment
of their bodies. And that men that bring forth
pageants that they play at the places that is
assigned therefor and no where else, of the pain
of forfeiture to be raised that is ordained
therefor, that is to say 40 shillings. And that
men of crafts and all other men that find
torches, that they come forth in array and in
the manner as it has been used and customed
before this time, nought having weapons,
carrying tapers of the pageants. And all
manner of craftsmen that bring forth their
pageants in order and course by good players,
well arrayed and openly speaking, upon pain of
losing of 100 shillings to be paid to the chamber
without any pardon. And that every player
that shall play be ready in his pageant at convenient time, that is to say at the mid-hour
between 4 and 5 o'clock in the morning, and
then all other pageants fast following each one
after other as their course is, without tarrying.

Players called for 4.30 a.m. and fined for in-
audibility—these two items alone give the flavour
of this mediæval stage.

CHAPTER II

IN spite of this vast amateur activity, which is to be traced throughout the length and breadth of Europe, the professional entertainers never quite lost their hold on the affections of the people. Almost all their work has perished, although one early English farce and several French farces give us an idea of their primitive repertory. They probably used no elaborate staging. A cart in a market square or a raised dais in a hall sufficed as of old for their purposes, and the ground on which they stepped, like the *platea* of the mystery cycle, became whatever locality they chose to call it. A curtain at their rear was no doubt useful, but when that was lacking those who were not taking part in the action could sit at the back of the stage and thereby become imaginatively invisible. As we come into the sixteenth century, we see the repertory of these players enlarging itself. The old farces continued popular, but out of the mystery cycle had sprung a fresh dramatic type, the morality, with which they were well qualified to deal. Many of these early moralities were planned, with suitable " doubling," for interpretation by four or five players, and their publishers

often laid particular emphasis on this fact when
they were setting out the title-pages. To say that
" four men might easily play this play " would be
likely to bring the text to the attention of these
professionals. Pictures of such companies have
been preserved in two dramas. Four or five
performers visit Elsinore to act before Lord
Hamlet ; the prince specifically welcomes their
leader, the bearded " heavy man," and " my
young lady and mistress," the boy who essayed the
women's parts. Further information appears in the
scene of entertainment introduced in *Sir Thomas
More*. More is acting as host to some friends
when announcement is made that several players
have arrived ; immediately he bids them enter.

> *Moore.* Welcome good freend, what is your
>   will with me ?
> *Player.* My Lord, my fellowes and my selfe,
> Are come to tender ye our willing service,
> So please you to commaund us.
> *Moore.* What, for a play, you meane ?
> Whom doo ye serve ?
> *Player.* My Lord Cardinalles grace.
> *Moore.* My Lord Cardinalls players ? now
>   trust me, welcome.
> You happen hether in a luckie time,
> To pleasure me, and benefit your selves.
> The Maior of London, and some Aldermen,
> His Lady, and their wives, are my kinde guests
> This night at supper. Now, to have a play,
> Before the banquet, will be excellent,

How thinke you Sonne Roper ?
Roper. Twill doo well my Lord,
And be right pleasing pastime to your guests.
   Moore. I pre thee tell me what playes have ye ?
   Player. Divers my Lord : *The Cradle of
      Securitie, Hit Nayle o' Th Head, Im-
      pacient Povertie,*
*The Play of Foure Pees, Dives and Lazarus,
Lustie Iuventus,* and *The Mariage of Witt and
      Wisedome.*
   Moore. The Mariage of Witt and Wisedome ?
   that my Lads,
Ile none but that, the theame is very good,
And may maintaine a liberall argument.
To marie wit to wisedome, asks some cunning,
Many have witt, that may come short of wise-
   dome.
Weele see how Mr. Poet playes his part,
And whether witt or wisedome grace his arte.
Goe, make him drinke, and all his fellowes too,
How manie are ye ?
   Player. Ffoure men and a boy Sir.
   Moore. But one boy ? then I see,
Ther's but fewe women in the play.
   Player. Three my Lord : Dame Science,
   Lady Vanitie,
And wisedome she her selfe
   Moore. And one boy play them all ? Bir
   Lady, hees loden.

This scene may be taken as an excerpt from life.
A Newe Interlude of Impacyente Poverte, a morality

play, was printed in 1560 with the characters arranged for four actors. John Heywood's *The playe called the foure P P* introduces four persons. R. Wever's *An Enterlude called lusty Iuuentus* has its characters arranged similarly to those in *Impatient Poverty*. My Lord Cardinal's men might also have included in their repertory *The Trial of Treasure* (five players), *New Custom* (four players), and half a dozen other known moralities.

This offspring of the religious amateur theatre, then, was being seized upon by the professionals, and necessarily in their hands it assumed new form. Not only were the characters cut down and rearranged, the comic portions received special attention, thus tending to remove it farther and farther from the sphere to which it originally belonged.

Meanwhile, the leaven of the Italian Renaissance was beginning to work in England. Men began to take a new interest in the classics of Rome and the world of Greece was opened before their eyes. From this came a new interest in the drama, and soon attempts were made, not only to revive comedies of Plautus in the original Latin, but to produce works in the vernacular based on these earlier models. Much of this activity was scholarly, most of it was purely amateur ; but the professional players, now growing in importance, were eagerly seeking for anything novel which they might add to their repertory, so that it is not surprising that they rapidly swept Terence and Plautus and Seneca into their net. Into it, too, they swept a heap of lore bound to be interesting to unsophisticated audiences—tales from the old romances, relics of Robin Hood, fragments of classical mythology, garbled historic facts, elements of the superstition of the folk. Out of all of these developed that Elizabethan drama which was to give us as its chief star the genius of William Shakespeare.

As decade upon decade advanced during the sixteenth century, more and more popular did this professional drama become and the number of men who devoted themselves to the " quality of playing " rapidly increased. Some were definitely retainers, the servants of rich lords ; others, even while nominally using the name of some nobleman or dignitary (as My Lord Cardinal's men did), were plying their artistic trade for their own profit. Until the latter part of the century they occupied no regular theatres but, following in the footsteps of their predecessors, took whatever platform opportunity suggested. So far as London was concerned, the inn-yards soon attracted their attention. Mine host welcomed them, for the performance of a play would be likely to mean many gallons of ale consumed ; the yard itself and the surrounding galleries provided adequate space for spectators of different social ranks and means, while a trestle stage could easily be set up at an end of the yard against one of the walls. At the Cross Keys and at the Bel Savage they established themselves for periodic " seasons," at the Bell and the Bull, at Whitechapel's Boar's Head

and Islington's Saracen's Head. The " seasons "
soon extended themselves, and at last several of
these inns almost lost their original function
and were transmogrified into permanent theatres.

With their settling down in one building and
thus abandoning their former itinerant performances, the actors soon bethought them of
erecting specially constructed buildings for the
presentation of their shows, and in this they were
aided by a number of men who, gifted with the
money that the players lacked, saw in the rapidly
developing drama an opportunity of adding to
their gains. By co-operation of this sort the first
permanent public theatre in London, styled
simply *The Theatre*, was erected in 1576 on a field
near Shoreditch. The choice of site no doubt was
conditioned by the fact that this land was just outside the city boundaries and so beyond the Lord
Mayor's control. This theatre continued to be
used for twenty-two years (till 1598), when its
timber served to provide the fabric of The Globe,
but the latent force in the professional world is
to be gauged by the sudden mushroom-like crop
of other theatres which sprang up in emulation of
that in Shoreditch. Within a year a rival house
had been opened as *The Curtain*, likewise in
Shoreditch ; a theatre at Newington Butts was
certainly complete in 1580 ; by 1588 *The Rose*,
on the south bank of the Thames, was causing
complaints from Puritanical neighbours. From
this time on, the region of Southwark became the
chief centre of professional activity. *The Swan*

was built there about 1595, and, most important
of all, *The Globe*, in 1598. Nor, in thus enumerating the chief public theatres erected before
1600, must we forget the so-called " private "
theatres. These were not private in the modern
sense, but were distinguished from the others in
that they were roofed in, originally used by child
actors and in the habit of charging a higher fee
for admission. The earliest private house was
that opened in *The Blackfriars* (1576) for the
children of the Chapel Royal. It was here in
later times that Shakespeare's company maintained their winter quarters. It must be remembered also, in dealing with these private
theatres, that the children were no less professional
than the adult actors ; at times, indeed (as Hamlet
tells us), even drawing away custom from the
major companies.

The men who built these theatres in London
were the groups of players who had developed out
of the small touring companies of the early sixteenth century. Although still theoretically vagabonds, they were becoming persons of considerable
importance. Within a few years Shakespeare and
others were to ask for, and receive, coats of arms,
and were to serve as Grooms of the King's
Chamber. In order to escape the toils of the
law, all these companies were, also theoretically,
" servants " of noblemen. Shakespeare's troupe
called themselves by the name of the Lord
Chamberlain, and later by that of the King himself.
The Lord Admiral's men, the Earl of Pembroke's

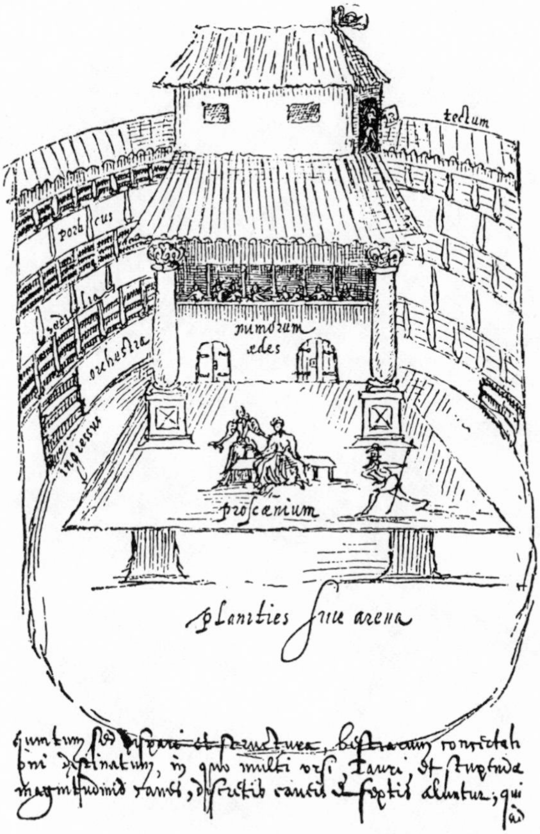
tectum
orchestra
ingressus
mimorum
ædes
proscænium
planities siue arena

THE SWAN THEATRE.
From a contemporary drawing.

men, the Earl of Sussex's men—these and a score
of others were acting regularly in Elizabethan
London. The noble attachment was rarely
anything but a fiction; it was retained, however,
until the eighteenth century brought new laws and
a change of tradition.

The great companies of players, being the direct
descendants of the jongleurs of the Middle Ages,
carried over with them the same general methods
of staging, modified though these might be by
fresh discoveries or by increased skill. As has
been seen already, there were two main methods
of presenting a play in mediæval times. Both of
these demanded the presence of an open unlocalized *platea*, but whereas one had no background save a possible curtain, the other employed
a series of mansions or pageants for certain localized
scenes, such pageants being independent and presenting many localities on the stage at one time.
The first type of setting was that used habitually
by the small companies of professional interlude
players; the other, taken over from the days of
the mystery cycles, probably with an influence
from the French actors at the Hôtel de Bourgogne,
was introduced into English Court performances.
The boy companies, being those most intimately
associated with the Court, seem to have patronized
this latter method of staging, while the adult actors
preserved, in an altered form, the simpler devices
of the earlier professionals.

Among the boys, then, the typical setting consisted of an open stage (the old *platea*), with a back-

ground composed of a series of realistic or symbolic
" mansions," these mansions indicating the various
localities which would be required in the course of
the play. Thus, had *The Winter's Tale* been
written, not for the Globe, but for the first
Blackfriars, it would have been produced with a
set of mansions representing Leontes' Palace, the
Temple at Delphi, a sea-coast, a pastoral landscape,
and a prison. These, with the help of the open
platea, would have been sufficient for the performance of the drama, and the action would have
proceeded from one portion of the stage to
another in accordance with the localities required
by the playwright. Obviously, this multiple
setting, or *décor simultané*, depends upon the convention that whatsoever localities are not in immediate use are made totally invisible to an
audience. That convention in itself is not an outrageous one, for the whole of theatrical art depends
upon conventions, and this is no greater than that
which allows modern spectators to suppose a lapse
of years while the orchestra plays its interval music
and gossiping voices raise a babble in the auditorium ; but, for this age, the simultaneous setting
presented one very serious difficulty. It definitely
put a restraint upon the free, romantic drama
which obviously appealed to the general public.
In the open-air mystery plays as many as thirty
different mansions could be set in a row at one
and the same time ; but in a small indoor theatre
such crowding of localities would clearly have been
impossible, and, above all other things, the new

drama that was arising in Elizabethan England demanded liberty and lack of outer control. Because of these aspirations, the *décor simultané* was avoided by the adult players and a separate system elaborated.

The methods of performance employed at the Globe (and other outdoor theatres) seem to have been based on a conscious or unconscious harmonizing of mediæval devices and of the newer humanistic aims expressed most forcibly in renaissant Italy. There the revived study of classical drama and of the classical theatre had led towards the adoption of a set of three standard sets used for tragedy, comedy, and pastoral respectively. Sometimes these sets were used independently of a formal proscenium arch ; sometimes such a proscenium arch was employed to mask the front of the set ; sometimes all was adapted to fit in to an architectural façade, itself based on the study of such antique relics as were to be found in the theatre of Orange. The most famous Italian playhouse of the last-mentioned type was the still-standing *Teatro Olimpico* at Vicenza, opened in the year 1584, and built by Palladio and Scamozzi. Here the stage consisted of a long and comparatively narrow platform, surrounded on three sides by a proscenium wall, heavily columned and ornamented. The two side portions of this wall were pierced by a couple of doors, while that portion which directly faced the audience had one large doorway in the centre and two smaller doorways, one on each side. In order to bring this "classical" façade into line with the more recent perspective art, the architects introduced at each of the five doorways a vista of streets, each slanting in such a way as to provide one clear line at one entrance for each member of the audience. In its stricter form, this setting of the Teatro Olimpico is more fettering than the *décor simultané* of France, for it allowed of no change of scene, and compelled the dramatists to place the whole of their fictional action in a market square or at the meeting of five roads ; but it was this type of setting on which, combined with the relics of mediæval methods, the principles of the adult stage in Elizabethan times were based.

In order fully to appreciate at once the likenesses and the differences between the typical Italian theatres of the sixteenth century and those of England during the same period, it is necessary to bear strictly in mind the open-air effects aimed at in the former. The " streets " of the Teatro Olimpico were supposed to meet in a *piazza*, or square ; the well-known tragic set of Sebastiano Serlio showed a wide open expanse shut in on three sides by palaces and temples ; the same artist's comic set similarly revealed a square with humbler dwellings, while his " satyric " scene displayed a pastoral landscape of rocks and trees and cottages. The interior setting at this period was entirely unknown in Italy ; only towards the end of the following century did baroque de-signers start to introduce into the theatre elaborate embellished palace halls and temple vistas. For

Frontispiece to *The Honest Man's Fortune*,
by Beaumont and Fletcher (1711), showing an
Elizabethan Hall with inner stage and balcony.

a single play, then, in Italy, one
locality served from the rising to the fa
curtain, any alteration of scene being
not with the regular tragedy or comedy, but with
the various spectacular *intermezzi*, or intermission
entertainments, which, precisely because of the
limitations imposed by the " unity of place " in
the drama itself, won so great a popularity among
contemporary audiences. These *intermezzi*, usually of a mythological or allegorical kind, freely
utilized the latest devices in scenic display and in
machine effects, but their wonders merely fettered
the more strictly the chains of classical control on
the tragic and comic dramatists of the period.

England, and with England the Spain of Lope
de Vega is to be associated, refused to acknowledge
any such restraint. A romantic drama was being
born, audiences for generations had become accustomed to the free manner of the interlude
staging, and classical preoccupations were not so
potent as in the country of Rome. No doubt
humanism had brought with it an interest in the
life and art of classical times ; no doubt, too, all
men looked to wonder-working Italy for inspiration and guidance ; but there was a fixed determination to make use only of such elements in
classical or in more recent renaissance art as might
accord with current needs and desires. In some
such way as this the Elizabethan theatre rose and
established its own conventions.

Of the professional outdoor theatres at the close
of the sixteenth century, the Globe, home of

Shakespeare, may be taken as typical. That play-house, reconstructable from the scattered evidence left to us, seems to have had a rounded auditorium, consisting of a ground floor innocent of benches (the " yard ") and at least two galleries fitted with rude seats. This seating or standing place occu-pied well over one-half of the entire circle formed by the walls of the theatre. Into the very middle of the " yard " jutted a large platform stage, with a railing at its edges, surrounded by spectators on three sides, and constituting the equivalent of the old *platea* and of the front portion of the acting space in the Teatro Olimpico. Even as early as the time of *Gorboduc* (1562) the temporary stages had traps (in that play three furies rise " from under the stage, as though out of hell ") ; and the professional Elizabethan theatre, we know, made full employment of this device. To the rear of the stage came a wall, perhaps ornamented with columns and architectural embellishment, and this was broken by three doors, one large and two smaller. Probably (and certainly in some theatres) another two doors appeared in the side walls, set at right angles to the back, and enclosing part of the platform. Above this the first gallery con-tinued round the whole of the circle, and provided both a place for spectators *behind* the performers and also an upper stage, which is suggested in two windows which originally appeared above the side entrances in the Teatro Olimpico. This main structure, accordingly, differs in principle hardly at all from the humanistic Italian form. Those

who built the Globe and those who played in it,
however, were not men likely to sacrifice freedom
and popular appeal to scholarly interest, and, as a
result, we find that the methods of performance
in the Elizabethan theatre depend on an entirely
different series of conventions from those employed in the Italian theatre.

In the first place, the platform, the *platea*,
might indicate any locality ; indeed, its flexibility
in this respect was as great as that of the mediæval
platea from which it sprang. " Go once or twice
about the stage," runs a direction in *Patient
Grissill* (1603), and in that simple peregrination
of the actors the audience imaginatively saw a
traversing of many miles. Its locality it always
took from the actors who stepped upon it. The
English soldiers in *Macbeth* make it into the
country surrounding Dunsinane ; the appearance
of Macbeth upon their exit immediately changes
the platform into the royal castle. At times this
stage might be localized for a whole scene by the
introduction of some simple pieces of property ;
a table and chairs would make it a tavern in East-
Cheap, and a tree in a tub would make it the Forest
of Arden ; but in the main no kind of visible
" scenery " was provided for the audience. On
the other hand, the adult actors had seen the
settings employed at Court, and they had recognized the value of an occasional scene definitely
localized by visible means, and as a result they
skilfully made use of that central doorway which,
in the Teatro Olimpico, had framed a perspective

vista. When the great doors were shut, then the platform stood as the whole stage; but when these doors were opened, the inner room thus revealed could show to the spectators a previously set interior, and here, perhaps, primitive scenery of a kind might be employed. This inner room might serve a variety of purposes: it could be a study for Dr. Faustus or a bedroom for Henry IV.; it could be a cavern in *The Tempest* and a throne-room in *Richard III*. Moreover, it could either be distinct from or blended with the outer platform. Sometimes it was the inner chamber in a house, and then the platform stood for the hall; sometimes a character would step from it towards the audience, and imaginatively he would thereby carry his locality with him.

Still further, the Elizabethans made use of that portion of the first gallery which was continued over the stage wall, using it as they used the platform, treating it as a kind of upper *platea*. In *King John* the citizens of Angiers might appear there and the gallery would immediately become the fortified walls of a city; in *Romeo and Juliet* the lovers might bid farewell on the gallery, and below the imaginations of the audience would see an Italian garden and above the balcony of a noble mansion. On other occasions, both doors and gallery could be brought into one stage picture. A character may knock at a lower door and another character from the gallery speak to him, the door and the gallery thus becoming the outside of a house, with entrance gate and first-storey window.

The use of platform, upper-stage, and inner-stage was flexible in the extreme, and the imagination of the audience was freely called upon. Thus not only might an inner scene, say of a bedroom, be revealed by the drawing of a traverse curtain or by the opening of the large central door and that inner scene be extended to include the platform, but a character might at will move to any portion of the acting area and still remain in a previously established *milieu*. In one episode, for example, a couple of men would make their appearance on the upper-stage which, by their words, took shape as the ramparts of a castle ; if need arose, then these same men could descend by an inner stairway, showing themselves again to the audience on the platform, and the platform then would assume the contours of the castle walls. To appreciate the system aright one must remember that precise locality really mattered little for the Elizabethan dramatists and their interpreters. Nowadays, we transform the texts of sixteenth century plays to approximate the image of modern dramas and carefully label each several scene with its exact locality. The audiences in the Globe did not trouble themselves to inquire whether this was a bedroom or a banqueting hall in a palace; so long as they saw a character indoors, that was enough. And for scenes outside, the barest indications were all they demanded. A wood, a field, a city street—these at most were required ; and for many episodes not even so much. The greater part of the Elizabethan dramatic action really takes shape in a place, or series of places, to which no more precise title can be given than " somewhere "—somewhere in England, somewhere in France, somewhere in Italy, these are the settings for a *King Lear*, an *As You Like It*, and a *Taming of the Shrew*.

It will be realized at once that this system of staging was one which provided the maximum of liberty both for playwright and for players, and in the light of this system we must read all the dramas of the period which were written for performance in the public theatres. According to present standards the scenes may seem to change too rapidly in such a tragedy as *Antony and Cleopatra*, but we have to remember that Shakespeare wrote this play, not for a series of pictorially indicated sets, but for a stage where only the appearance of a group of actors was required for the shifting of the theatrical locality from Alexandria to Rome, and where Cleopatra's monument was no heavily built up lath and canvas affair, but merely the gallery overhanging the platform below.

The Elizabethan public theatre still maintained many links with the theatre of the Middle Ages, and the conventions of both were fundamentally the same. The spectators who flocked to the Globe were in some ways not unlike their pre-decessors who had gazed open-mouthed at the mystery play in the market square. The people of mediæval times, as we have seen, had been content to imagine bare boards into Jerusalem,

but had refused to imagine that rib which was
later to be Eve. In the same way the Elizabethans
were willing to see in a stage-box the walls of
Angiers, but when it came to a death they
demanded that the actors should have bladders
full of blood all ready prepared to make a gory
show. Just as their predecessors took delight in
devils, so they crowded to see *Dr. Faustus*, and
took as keen a delight in the squibs as fourteenth-
century audiences had done.

Nor were they more exacting than these in
regard to costume. So long as an actor donned a
" Turkish bonnet " and sported a scimitar, he
was an Eastern character—no matter whether
Moor or ancient Dacian ; so long as he put on
a breastplate and carried a short sword, he was a
Roman soldier. In the performance of the mystery plays, as we saw, the basis of the costumes
employed, save for special characters, such as
devils, was contemporary dress, with little touches
introduced here and there to make class or time
or symbolic distinctions. If we simply transfer
this to the Elizabethan stage, we shall have some
idea of the way in which an *Othello* and a *Lear*
were originally performed. No doubt the methods
employed were very naïve, but there was something there which many modern theatres have lost
—stimulus for the imagination. So much is given
to us to-day that our imagination inclines to
slumber ; in the Elizabethan theatre it had to be
constantly on the alert.

Still another virtue the Elizabethan stage possessed : it brought the audience into intimate contact with the performers. In a modern playhouse we are separated completely from the stage action. An orchestral pit and a row of footlights keep two worlds apart. The Elizabethan theatre had none of this. The main stage (the relics of the old *platea*) jutted out into the very middle of the yard or pit, so that the actors who stood there were surrounded on three sides by the " groundlings." Nor was this all. Spectators often used the gallery which ran immediately above the central doorway, thus providing an audience behind the actors, while certain privileged youths with the wherewithal to pay for it had the right to draw their stools on to the stage itself and thus sit down within a foot or two of the performers.

At first sight it may seem as if this practice was an evil one, yet maturer reflection convinces us that it had its advantages. Certain critics may speak of theatrical illusion, but we know that in the theatre complete illusion can never be obtained. What the playhouse does give is imaginative illusion, whereby in *imagination*, and not in rational thought, we throw ourselves into the very spirit of the play that is being enacted before us. In the Elizabethan theatre the very proximity of the actors must have added to impression on the fancy. Hamlet was not a being in black posturing behind artificial footlights ; he was an Elizabethan gentleman who might, in happier circumstances, have been seated on the stool occupied by this or that young gallant. Falstaff was not a figure seen from afar ; he was a good boon companion jesting with the audience as if they—he and the spectators—were really at a tavern in East-Cheap. Recent productions of Elizabethan plays in their original settings and of modern plays in simplified intimate theatres have shown us how much we have lost from those days when Shakespeare watched the première of *Macbeth*.

Above all other things, this Elizabethan theatre was suited for the presentation of dramatic lines, and for these dramatic lines audiences gathered in the afternoons when the trumpet sounded to announce the time of performance. No doubt the actors were skilled in movement, able to dance a jig, engage in a wrestling bout or in a turn with the foils ; no doubt, too, these movements were eagerly watched and appreciated by the spectators. Music, song, and dance certainly played a considerable part in any Elizabethan stage performance. Any one familiar with the original quartos of the time will realize what an important rôle was taken by these elements. Kings enter to a " flourish " of trumpets, music plays during the " act-time," and, to record the words of Prynne,

by our owne moderne experience, there [is] nothing more frequent, in all our Stage-playes then amorous Pastorals, or obscene lascivious Lovesongs, most melodiously chanted out upon the Stage betweene each several Action ; both to supply that Chasme or vacant Interim which the Tyring-house takes up, in changing the Actors' robes, to fit them for some other part in the ensuing scene . . . as likewise to please the itching eares, if not to inflame the outrageous lusts of lewde Spectators.

For these spectators, lewd or not, Shakespeare made Bassanio choose his casket to music, to music set the whole last act of *The Merchant of Venice*, and opened his *Twelfth Night* with the pleasant sound of melody. Dances, too, were freely interspersed throughout the plays of the time, and it became common practice to end a drama with a " jig," which might at times be merely a comic step or two, but which more often became extended terpsichorean after-pieces notorious for their obscenity and including at least a modicum of rimed dialogue. Very popular were these, and by their skill in presenting them the English players on the Continent won no little esteem. As early as 1596 *Der engelländische Roland*, a jig adapted from the performances of some wandering troupe, was familiarly known.

But if part of the business of the players in Elizabethan times was to

Delight your eares with pleasing harmonie,

the harmony that audiences most admired was the harmony of words. Words were the true things of wonder and magic, and to these words spoken by the performers under the guidance of the

" book-holder " or prompter they listened in rapt attention. With the humanistic element in renaissance life, we must remember, had come a sudden awakened sense of verbal music ; words assumed a force they had never had in the past, and rhetoric came to be appreciated, not only for the conveyance of thought, but for its own sake. Men crowded to listen to marvellously ornate sermons and gained thence a passionate marvelling at excellent sentences rather than a reasoned admiration of good works. Oratory was a thing esteemed as a new-found wonder, and no better place for oratory might be found than the theatre itself. Maybe we of to-day, were we to be thrown back to Shakespeare's age, might find much in the histrionic method of that period to cavil at, but at least we should have been forced to recognize the able virtuosity of his players. From the conventionally composed and artificially delivered verses spoken by the first player in *Hamlet* tears might be wrung from the spectators, who, precisely because the stage on which that first player stood was not calculated to create an impression of reality, were prepared to exercise their imaginations in interpreting the conventional forms of utterance into terms of emotional life. Little as we know of the actual methods of performance in Elizabethan times, it seems certain that the greater tragic actors of the period were conventionally and oratorically inclined, and that the comedians erred similarly to the domain of farce. At the same time, one may believe that a marked difference was to be noted between the style of an Edward Alleyn and that of a Richard Burbage. Both may have been inclined towards rhetoric, but the latter's interpretation is likely to have displayed at once a greater refinement and a more pronounced moderation.

For Alleyn Marlowe wrote his " high astounding lines," and for Burbage Shakespeare created his Macbeth and Hamlet, Lear and Othello. The distinction between Tamburlaine and the Shakespearian heroes may well betoken the distinction between their histrionic styles. But both, be it repeated, were oratorical. Only at a time when sheer rhetoric appealed in the playhouse could dramatists have been summoned to pen such magnificent pieces of soliloquy and declamation as were provided by these two men. Faust's invocation to Helen and Tamburlaine's lyrical elegy to a departed Zenocrate were not intended as revelations of character ; they were, like the arias of opera, designed to form opportunities for the display of histrionic and rhetorical powers on the part of a tragedian. Maybe Shakespeare succeeded in infusing into these rich periods something which served to illustrate the workings of a human mind, but even in his plays perhaps we mistake when we endeavour to analyse a soliloquy as if it were wholly composed of rationally conceived psychological material. What Burbage wanted was a " fat " part, and a fat part in those days consisted in something he could " stick his teeth in." The " To be or not to be " soliloquy, and that other, " How all occasions do inform against me," unquestionably aid us in knowing Prince Hamlet better than otherwise we should have done, but their primal business was to provide an actor with lines fit for formal declamation.

Alleyn we may imagine as presenting a kind of statuesque appearance on the stage, Burbage as introducing more of mimetic action. Contemporaries saw in the latter the very embodiment of histrionic genius. " He's gone," cried a poet when he died :

Hee's gone, and with him what a world are dead,
Which he revived, to be revived so
No more. Young Hamlet, ould Heironymoe,
Kind Leer, the Greved Moore, and more beside,
That lived in him, have now for ever dy'de.
Oft have I seene him leap into the Grave
Suiting the person which he seem'd to have
Of a sadd Lover with soe true an Eye,
That theer I would have sworne he meant to dye.
Oft have I seene him play this part in jeast
Soe lively that Spectators and the rest
Of his sad Crew, whilst he but seem'd to bleed,
Amazed, thought even then hee dyed in deed.

The creator of these Shakespearian rôles and of many others born of Jonson's and Fletcher's imaginations must have been the Garrick of his time, and perhaps we shall gain no false idea of his style if we liken him to that later exponent of tragic and comic characters. In doing so, however, we must bear in mind that neither was a " naturalistic " actor. On the Elizabethan stage mimic action must have been of a decidedly conventional sort. Stage directions indicate that certain specific gestures were always demanded in certain situations. To show despair a character, like Romeo, throws himself violently on the ground, or, like Macduff, plucks his hat down over his brows, or, like Cassandra, ruffles his (or her) hair about the ears. Wringing of the hands is frequent, and the " passionate action " demanded of the Player-Queen in *Hamlet* must have been of an exaggerated sort. " Leave thy damnable faces and begin," cries Hamlet to her accomplice in crime.

The tradition set by Alleyn and Burbage was handed on to their successors, principally to John Lowin, whose professional career covers the years from the death of Elizabeth to the closing of the theatres in 1642. Identified with many Fletcherian heroes, he assumed, too, many of the parts that Burbage had essayed, and there is a Restoration tradition, referred to later in this book, that in some of these rôles he received instruction from Shakespeare himself.

Definitely related to the tragic were the comic methods of the period. The most famous actors of this kind in their day—a Richard Tarlton, a William Kemp, a Robert Armin—were clowns, what now we should have styled low comedy actors. Their merriment must have borne the same relationship to real life as did the tragic style of an Alleyn or a Burbage. Sometimes we wonder at the seeming crudity of Shakespeare's jesting, but this very crudity, we should remember, would admirably adapt itself to the often primitive and exaggerated methods employed by the far-ceurs who were to interpret his scenes. In the script the first lines of *Romeo and Juliet* are dull and pedestrian, but on the contemporary stage they must have furnished just such a medium as Kemp desired for his peculiar artistry.

Before leaving the Elizabethan theatre, we ought to observe one other thing. Until the Restoration in 1660 the English theatre knew no actresses. Boys, trained by the adult players, interpreted all the parts which to-day we associate with the personalities of a Mrs. Siddons or an Ellen Terry. That this was bound to have an impress upon dramatic composition cannot be doubted, and no particular ingenuity need be employed to discover the influence of these youthful actors upon Shakespeare's art. Of their histrionic style we have little contemporary evi-dence, but we may believe, from such few com-ments as have come down to us, that the skill of some succeeded in presenting adequate inter-pretation of feminine rôles. The whole stage was a conventional one—one which, in spite of a cer-tain realism demanded in details, deliberately de-parted, alike in comedy and in tragedy, from faith-ful transcripts of actual existence. Here acting was an art, and the æsthetic appeal of a performance lay, not in viewing the stage action as an excerpt from contemporary life, but in emotionally appre-

ciating the larger values which the playwright and
his actors were presenting in imaginative terms.
That is why the boy-players won such esteem
that they threatened the well-being of the adult
actors, why Ben Jonson could sincerely praise a
little Salathiel Pavy for his performances of old-
men's rôles :

> Weepe with me all you that read
>   This little storie ;
> And know, for whom a teare you shed,
>   Death's selfe is sorry.
> 'Twas a child, that so did thrive
>   In grace and feature,
> As Heaven and Nature seem'd to strive
>   Which own'd the creature. ·
> Yeeres he numbred scarce thirteene
>   When Fates turn'd cruell,
> Yet three fill'd Zodiaces had he beene
>   The stages iewell ;
> And did act (what now we mone)
>   Old men so duely,
> As, sooth, the Parcæ thought him one,
>   He plai'd so truely.
> So, by error, to his fate
>   They all consented ;
> But viewing him since (alas, too late)
>   They have repented.
> And have sought (to give new birth)
>   In bathes to steepe him ;
> But, being so much too good for earth,
>   Heaven vowes to keepe him.

Significant is it, when considering the skill of these boys in feminine rôles, that when Coryat, on his visit to Venice, " saw women act, a thing I never saw before," he could only comment that " they performed it with as good a grace . . . as ever I saw any masculine actor." On a modern stage a Desdemona interpreted by a boy would be an absurdity; on the Elizabethan platform at least one such Desdemona caused audiences to weep and aroused the thrilling wonder of impassioned tragedy.

This Desdemona, commented upon in the year 1609, was performing at Oxford ; and the record serves to remind us that London, although it was the centre of dramatic enterprise, possessed no absolute monopoly of play in the late sixteenth century. In town halls and on improvised stages throughout the whole of England the actors gave their touring repertoire. Some of these actors were merely provincial players, men (of secondary talents, unquestionably) who spent their whole lives in walking drearily from town to town in rapidly established circuits ; others were men of the major London companies who, driven from the city by plague or other misfortunes, sought to tide over a difficult period by country performances. No permanent theatres were established at this time in any other English town, but the very simplicity of the typical public playhouses of the metropolis permitted the wandering actors to adapt their action easily to whatever halls they might secure at their temporary places of sojourn.

Nor did they confine themselves to England. The *Englische Komödianten* soon won an international reputation, and even members of Shakespeare's company joined those many performers who carried knowledge of the English stage to Scandinavia, the Low Countries, Germany and beyond ; carried thither knowledge of the English stage and, we can doubt not, bore thence many concepts which, in drama and in theatre alike, were incorporated into the fabric of the playhouse in their native land.

CHAPTER III

SUCH influence from abroad, and particularly from Italy, increases as we step beyond the Elizabethan period proper and enter the reigns of James I. and Charles I. In Italy, as has been indicated, stage decoration did not stay long at the position it had reached in the Teatro Olimpico. The interest in perspective art and in cunning mechanism was too strong to permit the simple perspective vistas there to rule the world of the theatre. For a considerable time the classical tendency prevented the changing of scenes within the course of a tragedy or a comedy ; but from an early date such plays had been provided with *intermezzi* of a spectacular nature, and these *entr'acte* entertainments allowed full scope for the inventive activities of the scenic artists. Opera, too, began to grow in power and popularity, and, in spite of the fact that in origin the opera was a neo-classic experiment, soon it called in the services of the artists and the machinists.

The centre of this new stage craft was Italy, but Italian ideas spread rapidly throughout Europe, influencing the English no less than the French and German playhouses. In England no doubt the tendency and many of the conventions established by the Elizabethan public theatre persisted till the beginning of the nineteenth century, but gradually these conventions became harmonized with the newer ideas taken from Continental example.

In general these newer ideas may be summarily defined as the movement towards the proscenium arch and the picture-frame stage. Scene painting had appeared both in the French productions at the Hôtel de Bourgogne and in the English plays given at Court, but for these there was no change of scene and no attempt to secure a " realistic " or homogeneous picture ; indeed, the presentation of diverse localities on the stage at one time definitely prohibited such a representation. In the Teatro Olimpico there was the formal architectural façade with only narrow vistas through the doors of street scenes beyond. It is usually said that the first theatre of modern proportions was that playhouse at Parma called the Teatro Farnese, where the three main openings of the Teatro Olimpico were run into one, the result being a wide proscenium arch framing a scenic vista ; but the development of the proscenium arch had been hinted at years before in Italy itself, and was suggested at least in the typical public theatre of Elizabethan times. It would be more correct to say that many scenic artists and architects felt independently the need of having some framework for their stage pictures, and that popular taste was moving rapidly away from the set stage of the type represented in the Teatro Olimpico.

The new tendencies were acclimatized in England mainly through the activities of Inigo Jones. This man, a keen architect and an enthusiast for the theatre, had travelled widely in Italy and France, bringing thence many ideas which he proceeded to elaborate. The activities of Inigo Jones were confined almost entirely to the Court masque, a form of entertainment not directly connected with the public stage, but, in studying this masque, we have to remember that professional actors frequently took part in such shows, that masque-like elements began to intrude into plays from about 1608 onwards, and that once or twice at least Inigo Jones turned his attention to the stage production of regular dramas. The masque, therefore, and all the artistic activities connected with the masque, are intimately related to the fortunes of the English stage.

Inigo Jones was, above all other things, an experimenter. He wished to secure richness of setting and he wished to secure change of setting ; in seeking for these two things he tried many of the methods which were, even then, still only tentatively employed in Italy. For his first experiments he introduced the so-called *periaktoi*, triangular pieces of scenery with three separate faces, arranged on pivots in such a manner that they could be turned in order to reveal a change of setting. Sometimes effective, these *periaktoi* were, however, rather clumsy, and Jones soon abandoned them in favour of other and more easily handled devices. It would take up too much space here to

chronicle his gradual movement forward ; it is
sufficient to say that in the thirties of the seventeenth century he had established what was to
remain for centuries the stock type of scenic
decoration. For the masque of *Salmacida Spolia*
he prepared a series of settings which included
series of flat side wings running on grooves and
also a set of back " shutters " which could be
moved along with the side wings in order to reveal
a change of scene. With these side wings and
back shutters we are on the threshold of the
modern theatre ; indeed, the methods employed
by Jones are precisely those which may still be
seen employed by a number of provincial touring
companies.

For most of these groups of settings Jones built
a special proscenium arch, designed in such a
way as to be symbolic of the particular masque
for which it had been intended. In *The Masque
of Hymen* (1606) there were thus " two great
Statues, fayn'd of Gold, one of *Atlas*, the other of
Hercules . . . which were of *Releve*, embossed,
and tralucent, as Naturalls : To these, a Cortine
of painted Cloudes ioyned, which reach'd to the
upmost Roofe of the Hall ; and sodainely opening,
reveal'd the three *Regions* of *Ayre*." A formal
" arch " was used in *Microcosmus*, produced at
Salisbury Court theatre in 1637—indicative of the
way in which masque elements were carried over
to the public stage. For some of his shows Jones
utilized a painted curtain which either fell or was
raised at the beginning of the performance, the

arch thus revealed remaining open until the last act ; in none of his masque settings did he employ a curtain to mark a change of scene. Strangely enough, it was not until the eighteenth century that theatre workers came to use the front curtain regularly for these purposes of scene changing. That the " traverse " in the Elizabethan theatre almost served the purposes of the modern curtain is, of course, true ; thus in Legge's *Ricardus Tertius* (1580) " A curtaine being drawne, let the queene appeare in ye Sanctuarie, her 5 daughters and maydes about her . . ." which is what even that age called a " discovery." In *Albovine* (1629), " A Canopy is drawn, the King is discover'd sleeping over Papers " ; " Enter Bianca " in *Love's Sacrifice* (1633), " her hair about her eares, in her night-mantle ; she draws a curtain, and Fernando is discovered in bed sleeping " ; in *The Traitor* (1635) Amidea's body is " discovered on a bed, prepared by two Gentlewomen " ; and in *The Tempest* Prospero " discovers " Ferdinand and Miranda playing at chess. The use of the word " discovery," certainly, is comparatively rare in these plays, but even such directions as " Enter Francella as in a bed, asleep " (in *Brennoralt*, 1646), " Imogen in bed " (*Cymbeline*, 1609), and " Enter Leucippe (reading) and two maids at a Table writing " (*The Humorous Lieutenant*, printed 1647), refer to the employment of a similar device.

The curtain or traverse, however, was merely the one concealing the inner stage, and the application of this practice to the front curtain was not made during this time. For scene changes Jones himself often employed coloured lights to distract the attention of his audience, and later in the public theatres it was evidently quite usual to see the scene-shifters boldly moving away the unnecessary side wings in full view of the spectators. Even in an age when the passion for theatrical " realism " was growing in intensity, the older conventions persisted, and few, if any, sought to change them.

The masques presented at Court during the reigns of James I. and Charles I. were gorgeous affairs. Money lavishly was spent on this darling of the Court, and thousands of pounds expended on a single performance was considered in no way an outrageous sum. Happily we have two sources of information which serve in some manner to recall the vanished glories of the actual scene. The printed texts of the masques are lavish in stage direction, while at Chatsworth in the possession of the Duke of Devonshire there is still preserved a rich collection of the original designs for setting and costume executed by Inigo Jones and his assistants. These combined may provide us with the material for forming a mental picture of a Court performance in the early seventeenth century. As a first example, we may take the *Salmacida Spolia* of Sir William D'Avenant, presented on January 21, 1640. At the start,

A Curtayne flying up, a horrid Sceane appeared of storme and tempest ; no glimpse of

the Sun was seene, as if darknesse, confusion,
and deformity, had possest the world . . . the
trees bending, as forced by a gust of winde . . .
a farre off was a dark wrought sea, with rowling
billowes, breaking against the rockes, with rayne,
lightning and thunder.

A few moments later,

the Sceane changed into a calme, the skie
serene . . . in the Landskip were Corne fields
and pleasant Trees . . . with all such things as
might expresse a Country in peace, rich, and
fruitfull.

The third scene changed again to " craggy
rockes and inaccessible mountaynes." Then "the
further part of the Sceane disappear'd, and the
King's Majesty and the rest of the Masquers were
discovered, sitting in the Throne of Honour."

After a Song to the King, there came softly
from the upper part of the Heavens, a huge
cloud of various colours, but pleasant to the
sight, which discending to the midst of the
Sceane open'd, and within it was a transparent
brightness of thin exhalations, such as the Gods
are feigned to descend in.

This cloud itself eventually vanished and—

the Sceane was changed into magnificent buildings composed of severall selected peeces of
Architecture : in the furthest part was a Bridge

over a River, where many people, coaches, horses, and such like were seene to passe to and fro : beyond this on the shore were buildings in Prospective, which shooting far from the eye shewed as the suburbs of a great City.

From the highest part of the Heavens came forth a cloud far in the Sceane, in which were eight persons richly attired representing the spheares ; this joyning with two other clouds which appeared at that instant full of Musicke, covered all the upper part of the Sceane, and at that instant beyond all these, a Heaven opened full of Deities, which celestiall Prospect with the Chorus below filled all the whole Sceane with apparitions and harmony.

The picture thus presented may be supplemented by an analysis of Carew's *Cœlum Britannicum* (1633), produced at Whitehall a few years earlier. Here there was " a rich Ornament, that enclosed the Scaene " with a " Compartiment " at the top inscribed with the title of the masque. " The Curtain was watchet, and a pale yellow in panes, which flying up on the sudden, discovered the Scaene, representing old Arches, old Palaces, decayed walls, parts of Temples, Theaters, Basilica's and Therme . . . resembling the ruines of some great City of the ancient Romans, or civiliz'd Britaines."

This strange prospect detain'd the eyes of the Spectators some time, when to a loud Musick

Mercury descends ; on the upper part of his
Chariot stands a Cock in action of crowing :
his habit was a Coat of Flame colour girt to
him, and a white mantle trimm'd with gold and
silver.

Hereupon Mercury addresses the royal spectators. That finished, he is joined by

Momus attired in a long darkish robe all
wrought over with ponyards, Serpents tongues,
eyes and eares, his beard and hair party coloured,
and upon his head a wreath stuck with Feathers,
and a Porcupine in the forepart.

During their discourse

the Sceane changeth, and in the heaven is
discovered a Spheare, with Stars placed in their
several Images ; born up by a huge naked
Figure,

who is, of course, Atlas. By a charm various
monsters are summoned on stage—

The Lyrnean Hydra, the rough unlick'd Bear,
The watchful Dragon, the storm-boading Whale,
The Centaure, the horn'd Goat-fish Capricorne,
The Snake-herd Gorgon, and fierce Sagittar—

who " Dance in those monstrous shapes the first
Antimask of natural deformity." Down comes one
of the figures of the zodiac, "the skalding Crab,"

to dance a second antimask " in retrograde paces, expressing obliquity in motion." Others descend for a third antimasque, "expressing the deviation from Vertue," whereupon "All the Stars are quench'd, and the Sphear darkned." Soon after

Plutus enters, an old man full of wrinkles, a bald head, a thin white beard, spectacles on his nose, with a bunch back; and attir'd in a Robe of Cloth of gold,

and before him is danced "the fourth Antimask consisting of Countrey people, Musick, and Measures." He is followed by

Pœnia . . . a woman of a pale colour, large brims of a hat upon her head, through which her hair started up like a fury; her Robe was of a dark color full of patches; about one of her hands was tyed a chaine of Iron, to which was fastned a weighty stone, which she bore up under her arm.

In her honour "they Dance the fifth Antimask of Gypsies." Momus now calls on

Tiche . . . her head bald behind, and one great lock before, wings at her shoulders, and in her hand a wheel; her upper parts naked, and the skirt of her Garment wrought all over with Crowns, Scepters, Books, and such other things as express both her greatest and smallest gifts.

For her " they Dance the sixth Antimask, being
the representation of a Battle." Now Hedone
enters—

a young woman with a smiling face, in a light
lascivious habit, adorn'd with Silver and Gold,
her Temples crown'd with a garland of Roses,
and over that a Rainbow circling her head
down to her shoulders.

"They Dance the seventh Antimask of the five
Senses." This finishes the first part of the
masque ;

Atlas, and the Sphear vanisheth, and a new
Scaene appears of mountaines, whose eminent
height exceed the Clouds which past beneath
them ; the lower parts were wild and woody :
out of this place comes forth a more grave
Antimask of Picts, the natural Inhabitants of this
Isle, antient Scots and Irish ; these dance a
Perica or Marshal dance.

When this Antimask was past, there began to
arise out of the earth the top of a hill, which
by little and little grew to be a huge mountain
that covered all the Scaene ; the under-part of
this was wild and craggy, and above somewhat
more pleasant and flourishing ; about the
middle part of this Mountain were seated the
three Kingdomes of England, Scotland, and
Ireland. . . . At a distance above these sat a
young man in a white embroidered robe, upon

his fair hair an Olive garland with wings at his shoulders, and holding in his hand a Cornucopia fill'd with Corn and Fruits, representing the Genius of these Kingdoms.

The Kingdoms cry out to the mountain—

Open thy stony entralles wide,
And break old Atlas, that the pride
Of three fam'd Kingdomes may be spy'd,

and

At this the under-part of the Rock opens, and out of a Cave are seen to come the Masquers, richly attired like ancient Heroes, the Colours yellow, embroydered with Silver, their antique Helmes curiously wrought, and great plumes on the top; before them a troop of young Lords and Noblemens Sons, bearing Torches of Virgin wax; these were apparelled after the old British fashion in white Coats, embroydered with silver, girt, and full gathered, cut square coller'd, and round caps on their heads, with a white feather wreathen about them.

After their dance

the Rock with the three Kingdomes on it sinks, and is hidden in the earth. This strange spectacle gave great cause of admiration, but especially how so huge a machine, and of that great height could come from under the Stage, which was but six foot high.

" The Scaene again is varied into a new and pleasant prospect," showing " a delicious garden " belonging to " a Princely Villa." The Chorus enters now and addresses the Queen in song, and

the Song done they retire, and the Masquers dance the Revels with the Ladies, which continued a great part of the night.

The masque, however, is not yet done, for, at the conclusion of these " revels,"

there appeares coming forth from one of the sides, as moving by a gentle wind, a great Cloud, which arriving at the middle of the heaven, stayeth.

Two other clouds begin to appear beyond it; on one of them are seated Religion, Truth, and Wisdom, and on the second Concord, Government, and Reputation.

These being come downe in an equall distance to the middle part of the Ayre, the great Cloud beganne to breake open, out of which stroke beames of light; in the midst suspended in the Ayre, sate Eternity on a Globe. . . . In the firmament about him, was a troope of fifteene starres, expressing the stellifying of our British Heroes; but one more great and eminent than the rest, which was over his head, figured his Majesty. And in the lower part was seene a farre off the prospect of Windsor Castle, the famous seat of the most honourable Order of the Garter.

So eventually the night's festivities end with this delicate piece of Court flattery.

The above quotations have been presented in order to provide some idea—faint though that may be—of the wonders which Inigo Jones was able to put before the courtiers in the thirties and forties of the seventeenth century. He knew of scene-changing devices, of machinery, and of tricks in lighting, while his own artistic talents were by no means small. It is, accordingly, not to be wondered at that the masque should have become an exceedingly popular form of entertainment.

We are bound to believe, too, that, while the masque in itself was practically an amateur show, the stage glories devised by Inigo Jones were likely to make at least some impress upon the public stage. It is improbable that a courtly audience familiar with the Court wonders would have watched with anything save disdain and ridicule the primitive productions which many theatre historians postulate for the ordinary theatres, and we may be practically certain that the masque was making its influence felt in those playhouses during the reigns of James I. and Charles I. On the other hand, precisely how far these methods of scenic portrayal found their way

into the public theatres before the outbreak of the
Civil War in 1640 we cannot tell. The records
themselves are scanty and sometimes of a contradictory character, so that generalizations are
both difficult and dangerous. We have, however,
one or two sure facts to work upon.

The first is that extant plays originally produced
between about 1608 and 1620 show a decided
tendency to introduce more of a spectacular kind
than had been common in earlier years. Masque-
like elements intrude into the later plays of
Shakespeare—into *The Tempest* with its shepherds,
into *Macbeth* with its supernatural apparitions,
into *Cymbeline* with its eagle-borne Jupiter—and
such dramas as the component portions of Heywood's *Four Ages* indicate how the courtly
spectacularism was being exploited by a dramatist
who ever had his eye on the main chance. Gods
and goddesses make great show here, and supernatural ascendings are common :

Sounde a dumbe show. Enter the three
fatal sisters, with a rocke, a threed, and a paire
of sheeres ; bringing in a Gloabe, in which they
put three lots. Jupiter drawes heaven : at
which Iris descends and presents him with his
Eagle, Crowne, and Scepter, and his thunder-
bolt. Jupiter first ascends upon the Eagle, and
after him Ganimede.

Later " Jupiter appeares in his glory under a
Raine-bow " and " Medea with strange firey-

workes hangs above in the Aire in the strange
habite of a Conjuresse." Traps, too, are called
freely into play, so that "Neptune riseth dis-
turb'd" and "Hercules sinkes himselfe" while,
amid "flashes of fire . . . the Divels appeare
at every corner of the stage with severall fire-
workes."

Shows of this kind no doubt proved popular
amid those who had not the entrée to Court and
who, as a consequence, were ignorant of the richer
glories devised by Inigo Jones ; but Heywood's
effects, produced in an open-air playhouse, must
have been too crude to please the politer sort.
This bring us to the second item of importance
in this connection—the fact that, after the beginning of the century, the open-air public
theatre ceded its place to the indoor " private "
theatre. In 1600 *The Curtain*, an open-air house,
was built near Golding Lane, and that was followed
by *The Red Bull* (1605) in Clerkenwell and *The
Hope* (1613) in Southwark. When, however,
the King's men, chief company in London and
including Shakespeare among their members, in
1608 leased the Blackfriars theatre and proceeded
to make that their winter quarters, it was evident
which direction theatrical development would
take. The Red Bull and its companions fell in
esteem and proceeded to cater more and more for
lower-class popular tastes, while the more literate
and artistic spectators went genteelly to the Blackfriars or to *The Phœnix* (1617) in Drury Lane or
to *Salisbury Court* (1629). These indoor theatres

obviously permitted the use of scenic display much
more than the playhouses of the public type, for
here, apparently, no spectators sat upon the stage
itself. That it was possible for such theatres to
make use of scenery is proved by the fact that when
in 1636 the authorities at Oxford gave the Queen
permission to bring some specially constructed
scenes to her palace, a particular appeal was made
that the scenery might not be allowed to fall into
the hands of the common players. The very fact
that we do know of several plays presented in these
theatres with painted scenic effects compels us to
believe that the few such records we have of sceni-
cally displayed dramas (in the thirties of the
seventeenth century) were unique only in the
sense that the settings were a trifle more gorgeous
than those ordinarily presented.

These records, then, must be carefully interpreted as indicating, not the sole use of scenery
during this period, but the special shows which
won most popular attention. A proscenium arch
and five sets of scenes appeared in Nabbes'
Microcosmus at Salisbury Court in 1637 ; the same
year scenery was noted in Suckling's *Aglaura* at
Blackfriars ; and by 1640 Newcastle, presenting
The Country Captain without these embellish-
ments, was forced to apologize :

Gallants, I'le tell you what we do not meane
To shew you here—a glorious painted Scene
With various doores, to stand instead of wit,
Or richer cloathes of lace for lines well writ.

From this time on the word " scene " takes on a new significance.   The " scene magnificent " of Brome's *The Antipodes* (1638) refers to visual show, and even in 1633 Prynne, in his bitter *Histriomastix*, had authority for attacking the " common actors " with their " pompous and stately shows and scenes," now added to the " effeminate, rich and gorgeous attire," the " glittering and glorious apparel " signalized by theatre-haters from Elizabethan times.

All of this was bound up with a change in the audience.   By 1630 the motley Elizabethan crowd of spectators had given way to a fashionable assemblage of courtiers and their satellites, eager for any novelty and already familiarized with scenery at Court.   A gentleman of distinction is made to speak in Fletcher's *The Woman Hater* (1607):

I'll after dinner to the Stage to see a Play ; where when I first enter, you shall have a murmure in the house.   Every one that does not know cries " What nobleman is that ? "   All the Gallants on the stage rise, vail to me, kiss their hand, offer me their places : then I pick out some one whom I please to grace among the rest, take his seat, use it, throw my cloak over my face and laugh at him : the poor Gentleman imagines himself most highly grac'd, thinks all the Auditors esteem him one of my bosom friends and in right special regard with me.

More and more it was men like this who were attending the playhouses, and for such the things of a generation past were out of fashion—compared with Fletcher Shakespeare was dull :

> whose best jest lyes
> I' th' Ladies questions and the Fooles replyes :
> Old-fashion'd wit, which walkt from town to town
> In turn'd Hose, which our fathers call'd the Clown.

An age of gallantry and of aristocratic splendour was rapidly coming to the theatre.

The indoor playhouse in which this audience gathered and in which this scenery was displayed brings us appreciably closer to the modern stage. Indeed, it would not be entirely false or misleading to divide all the known theatres into two great classes—the open-air and the enclosed. In the Globe men were tied indefinably yet surely to the conventions operative in the Dionysian theatre of ancient Athens; in the Phœnix or Drury Lane of 1617 they were reaching forwards towards the Drury Lane of the nineteen hundreds. Once artificial lighting came to be employed there was opened up a line of development which previously could never even have been dreamt of. No doubt at first the full potentialities offered in the new conditions were not realized and the playhouse interiors were illuminated (as adequately as might be) in rude simulation of conditions present during the performance of plays out of doors ; in fact, such a method of illumination, with the auditorium as brightly lit as the stage, may be found still persistent in the middle of the eighteenth century ; yet these early " private " theatres of the seventeenth century contained all the elements which, elaborated and refined, have created our modern picture-frame stage and all its wonders of naturalistic and symbolic lighting.

Owning such theatres, the professional companies fully came into their own. The wandering interlude players, ever fearful of being arrested as vagabonds and vagrants, had grown into the great dramatic groups, and the earlier poverty-stricken members of some " four men and a boy " troupe had been replaced by persons of consequence, able, like Alleyn, to found important schools, and, like Shakespeare, to retire as landed gentlemen with real or fanciful coats-of-arms. The principal company of this age went by the name of the King himself (the former Lord Chamberlain's men), and besides these were several others which, although necessarily with less distinguished patronage and lacking such extensive traditions, catered for the aristocracy and their supporters. Numerous companies, it is true, were short-lived, but when one troupe disbanded another rose to take its place, and competition ruled.

What would have happened had not the Civil Wars driven theatres out of men's heads we cannot tell. This at least we know, that Sir William D'Avenant, courtier, poet, dramatist and masque-writer, reputed son of Shakespeare himself, had, in 1640, received from Charles I. a patent for the erection of an entirely new playhouse wherein ampler opportunities were to have been offered for the production of plays with the accompaniment of rich and elaborate scenery.

CHAPTER IV

THE RISE OF THE APRON STAGE : RESTORATION

THIS projected theatre of D'Avenant's remained for years a mere ideal, for, once the Puritans had seized control, no such amusements as stage-plays were permitted openly in London. It must not be assumed, however, that, because Parliament condemned the theatres, no plays were given in England between 1642 and 1660. The dramatic instinct had been too deeply fostered under the Tudor and Stuart monarchs for all traces of theatrical activity to disappear. In spite of peremptory laws, both actors and spectators dared the wrath of Puritan authority by arranging hasty performances in one or another of the now dismantled theatres ; sometimes these performances were interrupted by the soldiery, sometimes judicious bribes secured a peaceful termination. In the provinces, too, where often the Republican control was not so firmly established, the actors toured with their earlier repertoires, and at the annual fairs they presented their " drolls," * thus

---

* The droll was a short playlet made out of a portion of a longer drama. *Bottom the Weaver* was thus a droll which used only the low comedy elements of a *A Midsummer Night's Dream*.

78

keeping alive, not only the dramatic instinct, but the particular forms which that dramatic instinct had assumed in the early decades of the seventeenth century.

Apart from this, the " interregnum " of eighteen years was not of sufficient length to destroy the acting tradition. When the theatres opened again officially in 1660, one of the two principal troupes was composed almost entirely of men who had been boy actors in 1642 ; the other troupe was captained by Sir William D'Avenant, while a third and a fourth body of players were led respectively by William Beeston, who was old enough to have known Shakespeare, and by George Jolly, who, in the Puritan days, had travelled with his company of *Englische Komödianten* on the Continent.

Taking all these facts into consideration, it is manifest that, whatever outward break there was in officially licensed performances, in reality the Restoration stage was a direct development of the preceding Caroline stage. When the actors first recommenced their openly allowed activities, they naturally revived the old plays of Shakespeare, Jonson, and Fletcher, staging these on the antique platform stages on which many of them had been reared. The time, however, was ripe for change. Already, as we have seen, the masque scenery was having effect on regular drama in the earlier decades, and when, four years before the return of Charles II., D'Avenant succeeded in obtaining permission for the production of an " opera," *The Siege of Rhodes*, he summoned to his aid that John Webb who had been the chief assistant of Inigo Jones. The result of these twin forces, the one traditional and the other progressive, was that the new theatres built during the Restoration period mark a compromise between the Elizabethan and the modern. Both the Theatre Royal in Drury Lane and the Duke's Theatre in Dorset Gardens indicated the approach which was being made towards the Drury Lane and Covent Garden of to-day, yet both retained many features reminiscent of the Shakespearian Globe. The first *Theatre Royal in Vere Street*, used from 1660 to 1663, had no provision for scenery, but those which followed, the *Theatre Royal in Bridges Street* (1663–1672) and the *Theatre Royal in Drury Lane* (opened 1674), made free employment of scenic devices and of machines. D'Avenant's company had first made shift with *Lincoln's Inn Fields* (opened 1661), but by 1671 the demand for richer show had necessitated the erection of *The Duke's Theatre in Dorset Garden*.

While these theatres must have differed considerably one from another, the basic forms were sufficiently alike to permit of a general description covering all. An elaborate proscenium arch framed a " picture " made up of back shutters and side wings. In so far they were thoroughly modern. There was a pit in the auditorium, provisioned now with benches, and above that there were galleries, the lowest at least being divided into boxes. That contemporaries recognized the novelties which so freely were being

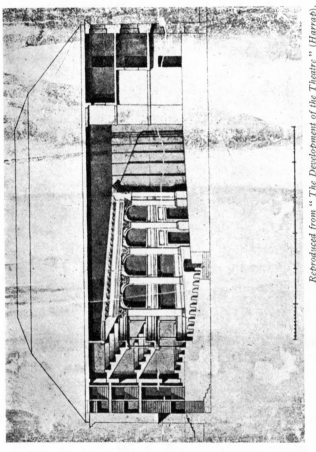

SECTION OF A THEATRE, PROBABLY DRURY LANE.

A design by Sir Christopher Wren, reproduced by permission
of All Soul's College, Oxford.

introduced into these playhouses is amply apparent when we survey the contemporary commentary upon the theatre. Even when the references to such novelties are satiric we may see what steps towards the later theatre had been made by the Restoration managers. No doubt with scenery and other refinements had come many follies, and with them elements of dramatic disintegration had been introduced, but the one must be accepted with the other. The prologue to Corye's *The Generous Enemies* (1671) notes both :

> Your Aged Fathers came to Plays for Wit,
> And sat Knee-deep in Nut-shells in the Pit,
> Course hangings then in stead of Scenes were
>   worn
> And Kidderminster did the Stage Adorn.
> But you, their wiser Off-spring, do advance
> To Plot of Gigg ; and to Dramatique Dance.

Here, however, the points of similarity give way to points of difference. In a modern theatre the stage stops short at the line of the proscenium arch, and the spectators are separated from the actors by a row of footlights and an orchestral pit. The Restoration audience and the Restoration actors, on the other hand, could not forget that platform of Elizabethan times, which brought those who performed and those who watched into intimate relation the one with the other. As a consequence, the theatre architects compromised, and carried the stage forward from the proscenium arch into the very middle of the pit. At the Theatre Royal, at least, the distance from the proscenium arch to the front of the stage was equal to that from the proscenium arch to the back wall of the theatre. And not only was there this architectural peculiarity. The actors themselves continued to perform as if they still stood on the old platform. Practically all the dramatic action took place in front of the proscenium, so that the rear part of the stage served merely as a pleasant pictorial background, against which the actors were outlined. If a performer was " discovered " (by the raising of the curtain) amid the scenery, he was always bidden to " come forward " before he started to speak.

In general, however, the actor was not so dis-covered ; usually he had nothing at all to do with the scenery, but entered in front of the curtain. For this purpose the architects of the Restoration theatres provided four or more so-called pro-scenium doors ; in other words, they set at each side of the arch a pair of ordinary doorways, with ordinary knobs and knockers, through which the performers might enter and make their exits, or which might, on occasion, serve almost as parts of the setting, as when a particular doorway was treated as the entrance to a fictional house. When this device was resorted to, another architectural feature of the Restoration theatre was called into service. Immediately above the four doors were four boxes, which thus looked down, not on the front stalls as in modern playhouses, but on the front part of the stage, or " apron." Spectators, undoubtedly, were sometimes seated in these boxes, but on occasion they could be used for the players' purposes. One character can knock at a door and another character speak to him from above, the side wall of the theatre thereby becoming the outside of a private house. In the next scene, the setting behind may represent a woodland glade, and immediately for the audience the proscenium doors and the boxes above disappear.

This, of course, is but a carrying over of earlier Elizabethan traditions and conventions, just as those had been, in turn, carried over from the mediæval period. Indeed, the best general impression we can make of the Restoration theatre is to be derived from a view which regards it as the link between the new and the old. Scenery had come to be the regular accompaniment of tragedy and comedy, but not only was the scenery merely a background for the performers standing on the apron, in itself it was often symbolic in character. Thus, in one play there is a scene of a fire. The action is supposed to take place in a city street, and characters rush in and out distractedly shouting and screaming in terror. A contemporary print shows us how this scene was presented on the stage. The characters in the street are there to the number of half a dozen, but, although they are supposedly in a street of the city, we see on a painted back cloth a distant view of the town itself. Painted flames and smoke are rising from it, and on its outskirts there are set stationary figures on the canvas, in attitudes of terror and dismay. Evidently contemporaries saw nothing peculiar in this admixture of in and out, of moving figures and of figures in arrested movement.

Nor did they see anything peculiar in another convention which carries us back to the days of the mystery dramas. In those dramas, it will be remembered, there was violent foreshortening of space. Thus, a character going from Jerusalem to Rome had but to make a few short steps across the *platea* in order to accomplish his journey. Now, however, change of scene has entered in, that change of scene being secured chiefly by the use of " shutters " or flats. Let us suppose that there is a full stage scene representing a prison. In it are the prisoner and two friends who have visited him. The next scene shows the outside of the prison buildings, and the two friends are supposed to have come from their unfortunate companion into the light of day. In a modern theatre, of course, the curtain would fall at the end of the first scene and rise to reveal the second. The Restoration managers rarely utilized the curtain in this way. Instead they commanded the two visiting friends to " move forward," leaving the prisoner at the back of the stage. Then the two flats on which was painted the exterior of the prison clicked together immediately behind them, thus shutting off the prison scene itself. All this, be it noted, was done in full view of the audience, so that the two friends, without moving an inch

after they had " moved forward," are made, as
on a wishing carpet, to journey from one locality
to another.

A similar convention is that wherein there is
shown a pair of flats painted to represent a wall
with a door. Some person of the play enters and
calls to another person within. Receiving no
reply, he knocks on the door and demands that
it should be opened. As the next scene is supposed
to take place *within* the other room, the flats are
then bodily withdrawn ; the person who had been
without says, " See ! he has opened the door.
Let us go in," and at once starts talking as if he
were entered into the inner chamber. The
spectators of the Restoration period, precisely
because they were directly descended from the
spectators of Elizabethan days, accepted such conventions without a word of protest.

Many individual features of the Restoration
playhouse likewise are to be traced back to the
Globe and the Fortune. In those theatres the
orchestra had habitually performed in the " music-
room," evidently one section of that gallery which
extended over the back wall of the stage. If we
turn to the picture of the proscenium arch at
Dorset Garden as engraved in Settle's *The Empress
of Morocco* (1673), we see, at the very top of the
arch, and consequently immediately behind the
proscenium, a large box with windows. Round it
and below it are painted various instruments of
music. It is the place of the orchestra. Undoubtedly, Killigrew, master of the Theatre Royal,

did attempt in 1663 to place the musicians
" below " the stage, but Pepys probably voiced
contemporary opinion when he declaimed against
the experiment. " The house," he says, " is made
with extraordinary good contrivance, and yet hath
some faults, as the narrowness of the passages in
and out of the pitt, and the distance from the
stage to the boxes, which I am confident cannot
hear ; but for all other things it is well, only,
above all, the musique being below, and most of it
sounding under the very stage, there is no hearing
of the bases at all, nor very well of the trebles,
which sure must be mended."   Killigrew evidently
was forced to return to his earlier practice, for a
ballad which describes the burning of the Theatre
Royal at a later date relates how the flames rise
upward to the first gallery, lick their way up the
sides of the proscenium, and eventually reach the
music box itself.   It was not, indeed, until the
eighteenth century that a pit was arranged for
the musicians immediately in front of the first
rows of ground-floor seats, the English " stalls "
and the American " orchestra."

In spite of the forward apron and of the con-
tinuation of Elizabethan acting conventions, the
Restoration playhouse was built for the display
of scenery ; indeed the tendency was progressive,
and what the earlier Theatre Royal could introduce
was no longer satisfactory in 1671 when the Dorset
Garden house was erected to meet the increased
demands for show and spectacle.   The poet-
dramatists groaned and penned satiric verses, but

all to no avail. .The King's men, having not the wherewithal to compete adequately with the Duke's company, commissioned Dryden to pen a prologue (1674) apologizing for their " plain built house," and at the same time protesting that dramatic lines were of more importance than richness of scenery. " We in our plainness may be justly proud," Dryden makes them say, and attacks the reign of " scenes, machines, and empty operas." The audience, however, must have listened with greater approbation to Shadwell's prologue, spoken at the Duke's Theatre when an operatic *Tempest* was produced.

Acknowledging the truth of Dryden's strictures, namely that the managers of the Duke's Theatre had expended huge sums of money on their shows, Shadwell protests that in doing this the company was but moving with the times and accuses the Theatre Royal of niggardliness :

> Had we not for your pleasure found new wayes,
> You still had rusty arras had and thred-bare playes ;
> Not scenes nor Woomen, had they had their will,
> But some with grizl'd Beards had acted Woomen still.

The epilogue laughingly followed in similar strain :

> When you of Witt and sence were weary growne,
> Romantick, riming, fustian Playes were showne ;

We then to flying Witches did advance
And for your pleasures traffic'd into France.
From thence new acts to please you we have
     sought.
We have machines to some perfection brought,
And above thirty Warbling voyces gott.
Many a God and Goddesse you will heare,
And we have Singing, Dancing Devils here—
Such Devils, and such gods, are very Deare.

Some idea of the scope of this lavish scenic embellishment is to be obtained from the stage directions in various " dramatic operas " of the time.   One of these was *The Fairy Queen* (1692), adapted from *A Midsummer Night's Dream*.   In the third act the scene, changing, shows " a great wood " :

A long row of Trees on each side : a river in the middle : Two rows of lesser Trees of a different kind just on the side of the River, which meet in the middle, and make so many Arches : Two great Dragons make a Bridge over the River ; their Bodies form two Arches, through which two Swans are seen in the River at a great Distance. . . . While a Symphony's playing, the two Swans come swimming on through the Arches to the Bank of the River, as if they would land ; there turn themselves into Fairies and Dance ; at the same time the Bridge vanishes, and the Trees that were Arch'd raise themselves upright. Four Savages

Enter, fright the Fairies away, and Dance an
Entry.

As if this were not enough, the fifth act introduces a peacock machine bearing the goddess
Juno :

> While a Symphony plays, the Machine moves
> forward, and the Peacocks spread their tails,
> and fill the middle of the Theatre. Juno sings ;
> the Machine ascends. While the Scene is
> darken'd, a single entry is danc'd ; then a
> Symphony is play'd ; after that the Scene is
> Suddainly Illuminated, and discovers a trans-
> parent Prospect of a Chinese Garden ; the
> Architecture, the Trees, the Plants, the Fruit,
> the Birds, the Beasts quite different from what
> we have in this part of the World. It is ter-
> minated by an Arch, through which is seen
> other Arches, with close Arbors, and a row of
> Trees to the end of the View. Over it is a
> hanging Garden, which rises by several ascents
> to the Top of the House ; it is bounded on
> either side by pleasant Bowers, various Trees,
> and numbers of strange Birds flying in the Air,
> on the Top of a Platform is a Fountain, throwing
> up Water, which falls into a large Basin.

We may credit the truth of Downes's statement
that " the Expences in setting it out " were very
great, so that although " the Court and Town were
wonderfully satisfy'd with it," the company pro-

fited little. We may, too, appreciate the dramatist's complaint :

> Then came Machines, brought from a Neighbour
>   Nation—
> Oh, how we suffer'd under Decoration !

" The   Court   and   Town   were   wonderfully
satisfy'd with it "—this phrase of Downes must
lead towards a consideration of the auditorium
arrangements and of the characteristics of the
spectators during this period. The modern stalls
were unknown until the first half of the nineteenth
century. The whole floor of the Restoration house
formed the pit, set with backless benches, which
in some theatres were covered with green baize.
This was the portion of the theatre most frequented by the wits and the beaux ; it was to the
denizens of these regions that poets usually addressed their piteous appeals and their vainglorious
boasts in prologue and in epilogue. Immediately
above this, and raised only a few feet above the
back seats of the sloping pit, came the first gallery,
which ended in the boxes overhanging the apron
stage. This was the select position of the aristocracy, particularly of the ladies of the Court, whose
beauty and whose refulgent eyes often attracted
attention from the stage. The King's box was
here at the very centre of the gallery, and it was
during the performance of a play that William
Wycherley the dramatist had his first conversation
with the Duchess of Portsmouth. She was seated
in the royal box, and he in the last bench of the

pit. Above this, in turn, was the upper gallery, the haunt of middle-class people (such as frequented the playhouses), of courtesans, and of footmen.

This audience in a Restoration theatre differed very markedly from a typical playhouse audience of to-day. In discussing the theatre of the Restoration it has to be remembered that the great mass of the people had inherited the prejudices of their Puritan forefathers, and, while they might be content politically to accept a return to royalty, they were not prepared morally to sacrifice the opinions for which men had fought a few years previously. The result was that the theatre became practically a thing of the Court. The two companies of players were known as the "servants" of the King and of the Duke of York respectively, and the first, at least, had the privilege of wearing and of receiving by grant State livery. Charles II. himself took a close personal interest in the fortunes of the actors. His coronation suit was lent on one occasion for the performance of a play. This was D'Avenant's *Love and Honour* ; Downes, the old prompter, records that it was

> richly Cloath'd, the King giving Mr. Betterton his Coronation Suit . . . the Duke of York giving Mr. Harris his . . . and my Lord of Oxford gave Mr. Joseph Price his.

Others followed the royal fashion, and even the Court ladies showered their favours on the stage.

Mrs. Barry on occasion wore the Duchess of York's wedding dress in a play, and when that princess became queen she bestowed on the same actresss her robes of coronation.

Charles's interest in the playhouses was a lively one, and he did not hesitate to make suggestions and issue commands. The Earl of Orrery records how the King proposed to him the writing of a play in rimed verse; the King it was who brought a Spanish play to the notice of Sir Samuel Tuke, who made out of it *The Adventures of Five Hours*, and who caused John Crowne to become acquainted with another Spanish comedy, the basis of *Sir Courtly Nice*. Even the actors were guided by him. In 1663 Pepys observed that " by the King's command, Lacy now acts " the principal rôle in *The Humorous Lieutenant* " instead of Clun." When troubles threatened he exercised his royal prerogative; the famous Union of the Companies in 1682 seems to have been largely due to him. At the theatre his attendance was regular, and from one he took the most famous of his mistresses, Nell Gwyn.

With this personal interest of Charles, it was natural that the courtiers, who watched his every movement, should flock gaily to the play; and it was these courtiers, with their satellites, who formed the greater part of the theatre audiences of the time. How small a proportion of the population of London frequented the playhouses is seen by the facts that from 1662 to 1682 only two theatres could exist, that their existence was

of such a precarious kind as to demand amalgama-
tion, and that from 1682 to 1695 one theatre alone
served the needs of London's play-going public.
If further evidence be required it will be found in
The Term Catalogues, the booksellers' publishing
lists for the Restoration period. There newly
issued volumes were listed in class divisions, and
even a casual glance at any few of these advertisements will demonstrate the small place occupied
by the drama. The very first (for Michaelmas
term, 1668) gives fifteen books of divinity, five in
the section of " physick," eight in that of history,
and five in that of " humanity " ; against these
are to be set only five plays. The following term
not one new play is recorded, while the list for the
next (Easter, 1669) gives only three. There was
a large reading public during those years, but the
greater part of it confined attention to Expositions
of the Book of Job, Lives of Archbishop Laud,
and Epitomes of the Art of Husbandry. Plays
were issued in small editions and were perused
only by a few hundred courtiers.

It is therefore not surprising that the playhouse became, during the latter half of the seventeenth century, a playhouse in more than one sense
of the term. The ostensible purpose of the theatre
was still the producing of comedy and tragedy,
but the audience of courtiers who were in regular
attendance came there, not only to see, but to be
seen. In other words, they regarded the theatre
as a kind of club where they could meet their
friends and converse wittily on the affairs of the

day. A gentleman in those times might frequent the playhouses on " tick " ; if he cared, he might enter the pit for half an hour without making any payment at all. Should he find the play uninteresting—still more to the point, should he find there no witty companion or pleasing mistress—he could strut out once more to seek for enjoyment outside.

The babel of conversation in a Restoration theatre during the very performance of a drama is something which we to-day must find it difficult to imagine. Pepys often chronicles the conversations he heard there—chronicles, too, the impertinent remarks made by Sedley or another on the action and language of the piece put forward on the stage. Should a quarrel break out between two courtiers in the pit—a not uncommon occurrence—the mimic story would be lost, and a real duel might well take the place of imaginary combats. One gentleman, we know, thus perished during an interrupted performance of *Macbeth*. In reading the plays of the Restoration period—whether they be bombastic tragedies of the heroic sort or else witty comedies of manners—these characteristics of the spectators must be carefully borne in mind.

It was during the period of the Restoration that there was established that dual control of the stage which lasted for over a century, and the influence of which operated even in the reign of Queen Victoria. After a few months of chaos, Charles II. granted to Sir William D'Avenant and to Thomas Killigrew a complete monopoly in London theatrical affairs, issuing two patents which were handed down to the managers of the nineteenth century. The one company (D'Avenant's) was styled the Duke's, the other (Killigrew's) went by the name of the King's Men. D'Avenant evidently considered himself heir to the play property of many pre-war companies, and as clearly the King's Men looked back to that company to which Shakespeare had belonged and to which James I. had given his patronage. The latter occupied the Theatre Royal, which was the ancestor of Drury Lane ; the former played at a theatre in Lincoln's Inn Fields, and later in the ornate Duke's house in Dorset Garden. Amalgamating, as we have seen, in 1682, the companies split once more in 1695, when Betterton seceded on account of differences with the managers.

The word " managers " reminds us that this granting of patents to D'Avenant and Killigrew introduced still another fresh tendency in the English stage. Not only was a monopoly now first established, but the system of managerial control was also introduced. A move in this direction had been made before the Civil Wars when Charles I. granted D'Avenant a patent to " govern " as well as " entertain and keep " a company of actors, commanding these actors to " follow his orders and directions," but the theory was not really carried into practice until after the Restoration. The Elizabethan companies had been free, democratic bodies, associations of players who all held shares in the building, in the properties and in the stock of dramas. These men, after paying the expenses incurred by their performances, including the salaries given to the non-sharing actors whom they had to make use of on occasion (the " hirelings "), divided their profits according to the amount of shares each held. For the most part, the sharers remained as permanent members of their troupes ; there was even an undefined but nevertheless effective system for the payment of pensions either to those who were retiring on account of old age or to their dependents on death. Any official responsible for financial or artistic control was an appointee of the body corporate, and the "manager," in the modern sense of the term, was unknown. By the action of Charles II., on the other hand, D'Avenant and Killigrew were made "masters" of their companies. They and they alone had the right and power to engage actors, to arrange salaries, to select plays for performances. True, in a modified way the sharing system continued, but gradually that too disappeared in favour of one by which actors were engaged on salary. During the last years of the century Betterton and his wife were drawing a weekly £5 from the treasury.

Judging from the accounts of contemporaries (our only means of gauging histrionic worth), these companies seem to have been brilliant, although, perhaps, our ears—could we now listen to the antique histrionic tones—would not much relish the full-blooded rhodomontades which were apparently associated in those times with the heroic drama. Above all the other actors stands Thomas Betterton, excellent, according to contemporaries, both in tragedy and in comedy, a stalwart figure and one of considerable majesty, who dominated the stage till the early years of the eighteenth century. Trained in D'Avenant's company by those who had had experience in acting before 1640, he carried on the tradition that had been set in Shakespeare's time. The general continuity of tradition, indeed, is a thing we must ever bear in mind at this period lest we fall into the error of regarding the Restoration playhouse as something entirely distinct from the playhouse of the Elizabethans. Betterton, we are informed by Downes, was particularly effective in *Henry VIII.*; he had been " Instructed in it by Sir William [D'Avenant], who had it from Old Mr. Lowen, that had his Instructions from Mr. Shakespear himself." Whatever truth there is in the record, at least it indicates the way in which that age looked back for inspiration to the great age that had gone. Not that it was prepared to admit any inferiority ; following these remarks on Henry VIII., Downes hastens to add that he " dare, and will aver that none can or ever will come near" Betterton "in the performance of that part." Betterton's genius seems ably to have harmonized with that which produced the tragic heroes of the " love and honour " drama, a fact which led him to introduce an element of exalted seriousness into his treatment of Shakespearian rôles. " As Hamlet," remarks Aston, "when he threw himself at Ophelia's feet, he appeared a little too grave for a young student, and his repartees seemed rather as apothegms from a sage philosopher than the sporting flashes of a young Hamlet." Yet to Cibber such faults weighed little. " Betterton," he believes, " was an Actor, as Shakespear was an Author, both without Competitors ! "

You have seen a Hamlet perhaps, who, on the first Appearance of his Father's Spirit, has thrown himself into all the straining Vociferation requisite to express Rage and Fury, and the House has thunder'd with Applause ; tho' the mis-guided Actor was all the while (as Shakespear terms it) tearing a Passion into Rags. . . . For you may observe that in this beautiful Speech, the Passion never rises beyond an almost breathless Astonishment, or an Impatience, limited by filial Reverence, to enquire into the suspected Wrongs that may have rais'd him from his peaceful Tomb ! and a Desire to know what a Spirit so seemingly distrest, might wish or enjoin a sorrowful Son to execute towards his future Quiet in the Grave ? This was the Light into which Betterton threw this Scene ; which he open'd with a Pause of mute Amazement ! then rising slowly, to a solemn, trembling Voice, he made the Ghost equally terrible to the Spectator, as to himself !

A dominating figure, Betterton bestrid the stage from the first year of Charles II.'s reign to the early eighteenth century, sustaining most of the great Shakespearian rôles (not only Macbeth and Hamlet, but Sir Toby Belch and Mercutio as well), besides creating a variety of important characters in contemporary drama, from Lord Beaufort in Etherege's *A Comical Revenge* and Ramble in Crowne's *The Country Wit* to Alphonso in Dryden's *Love Triumphant* and Fainall in Congreve's *The Way of the World*.

Betterton, however, stood not alone. Many gifted companions and rivals he had, and there were some in that time who even preferred them to him. Mohun of the King's company won considerable fame. Already acting women's rôles in Beeston's company about 1637, he appeared in several Fletcherian parts on the organization of Killigrew's troupe. He was a noted Iago and created Bellamy in Dryden's *An Evening's Love* and Hannibal in Lee's *Sophonisba*. Henry Harris was Horatio to Betterton's Hamlet, Aguecheek to his Sir Toby Belch. Until his retirement in 1684 he, too, was a popular figure, being particularly praised by Downes for his Cardinal Wolsey. The career of Charles Hart of the King's men covered much the same years (1660–1683). Hotspur in *Henry IV.*, Othello, Mosca in Jonson's *Volpone*, Brutus in *Julius Cæsar*, were among his praised rôles ; he was the original Celadon of *Secret Love* and the Palamede of *Marriage à la Mode*.

Somewhat later in time came William Powell, one, too, of Betterton's rivals, who, according to Aston, embraced the more exaggeratedly bombastic style—he "outrav'd all probability, outheroding Herod, while Betterton kept his passion under, and shew'd it most (as flame smoaks most when stifled)." Kynaston in dignified rôles was richly praised by Cibber, and Sandford in those of villains—the latter " an excellent Actor in disagreeable Characters."

Comic actors, as might be imagined from the vogue of the contemporary comedy of manners, likewise abounded. The fine gentleman, the polished gallant who made " the wit of the poet " seem " always to come from him extempore," was Mountfort, a man who appears to have excelled by his brilliance. " He fill'd the Stage," remarks Cibber, " not by elbowing, and crossing it before others, or disconcerting their Action, but by surpassing them, in true and masterly Touches of Nature." Specializing in high comedy, he had as companions a James Nokes, a Thomas Doggett, a Joe Haynes, and a John Lacy. Nokes was the simple low comedian. The very sight of him on the stage provoked a laugh, and " the louder the Laugh, the graver was his Look upon it ; and sure, the ridiculous Solemnity of his Features were enough to have set a whole Bench of Bishops into a Titter." " When," continues Cibber,

he debated any matter by himself, he would shut up his Mouth with a dumb studious

Powt, and roll his full Eye into such a vacant Amazement, such a palpable Ignorance of what to think of it, that his silent Perplexity (which would sometimes hold him several Minutes) gave your Imagination as full Content, as the most absurd thing he could say upon it.

Doggett revelled in characters like Sancho Panza of D'Urfey's *Don Quixote*—" a little, lively, spract man," as Tony Aston describes him, the mercurial Bottom to Nokes's Dull. Haynes danced and sang and grimaced through his clowns and grotesques. In Falstaff, in Teague of *The Committee* and Sauny of *Sauny the Scot* (an adaptation of *The Taming of the Shrew*), Lacy made many memorable essays in comic business. One other similar performer, too, won much praise in this time—Cave Underhill, who excelled in blockheads and boobies. " His Face was full and long," Cibber tells us ;

from the Crown to the end of his Nose, was the shorter half of it, so that the Disproportion of his lower Features, when soberly compos'd, with an unwandering Eye hanging over them, threw him into the most lumpish, moping Mortal, that ever made Beholders merry !

That all these men were truly gifted we cannot doubt, and we may safely assume that an Otway and an Etherege found talented exponents for their masterpieces in dramatic literature. Complaints there are during these years concerning histrionic representation, but such seem to be directed rather at carelessness than at lack of talent.

The actors must, in this period, be considered in close connection with the spectators, for in these club-room theatres of the Restoration there was far greater intimacy between the stage and the auditorium than is possible to-day. We may have now followings for particular actors and actresses, but the stock companies of the seventeenth century were more fixed than our present-day theatrical companies, and as a consequence the audience came to know the actors, both on the stage and off, in an intimate way alien to our theatre. Parts were cast on a type plan ; the low-comedy actor was always the low-comedy actor, and the villain remained always the villain. The drama-tists, recruited out of the select body of spectators, knew exactly those persons who could appear in their comedies or tragedies, and accordingly wrote with particular performers in their mind's eye. The uniformity of Restoration drama is thus to be explained just as a similar cause must be sought for the sameness in early nineteenth-century farce and melodrama.

To the period of the Restoration belongs the introduction of the professional actress to the English stage. In the mediæval drama women certainly did appear occasionally, but even Eve in the Garden of Eden before the Fall was more commonly portrayed by a man. The Elizabethan stage knew no actresses, even although those many English travellers of the time were able to bring back to London accounts of feminine acting on the Continent. By 1660, however, the time was ripe for change, and history was in the making when, presumably on December 8 of that year, an actor stepped forth on the boards of the old Theatre Royal in Vere Street and, before a performance of *Othello*, addressed the audience prologue-wise :

> I come, unknown to any of the rest,
> To tell you news—I saw the Lady drest ;
> The Woman playes to-day, mistake me not,
> No Man in Gown, or Page in Petty-Coat ;
> A Woman to my knowledge. . . .
>   In this reforming age
> We have intents to civilize the Stage.
> Our women are defective, and so siz'd
> You'd think they were some of the Guard dis-
>   guiz'd ;
> For (to speak truth) men act, that are between
> Forty and fifty, Wenches of fifteen,
> With bone so large, and nerve so incomplyant,
> When you call Desdemona, enter Giant.

And history was in the making, too, when, the epilogue advancing and making inquiry—

> And how d'ye like her ? . . .
> But, Ladies, what think you ? For, if you tax
> Her freedom with dishonour to your Sex,
> She means to act no more, and this shall be
> No other Play but her own Tragedy—

applause greeted this unknown's first essay and the actress was established. Established, at least, in theory, for in fact several years were to elapse before trained performers were secured to enact all feminine rôles. Edward Kynaston continued to play his Epicoene (Jonson's *The Silent Woman*) and his Evadne (Fletcher's *The Maid's Tragedy*) for some time after the delivery of this prologue and epilogue—only abandoning these rôles for Antony and Cassio when the Mistress Hughes and Mistress Knepps had found their ways backstage.

The introduction of the actress was no fortuitous innovation, for the Restoration period is marked, above all other things, by a changed view of womankind. For the first time in English history, women came to take a place in life alongside of men. The appearance of the first professional woman writer in Mrs. Aphra Behn was no extraordinary thing ; the tone of the comedy of manners reflects fully—indeed, could not have come into existence without—the frank equality shared by the sexes. It is no wonder, then, that the end of the seventeenth century saw the introduction of the actress to the stage ; and, once the pioneer effort had been made, clearly the actress had to stay. Not only did she provide better interpretation of feminine rôles in old plays and in new, but she gave an added thrill of interest to the members of the club-house theatre. The gallants, it is to be feared, often came to see a pretty Mistress So-and-so rather than to listen to the play, and the career of the lively Nell Gwyn may be taken as typical of many another actress's life during this time. Whatever scandals the actresses caused, however, the fact that they had come to the stage marks out the Restoration period as the beginning of the modern theatre, and it is to be observed that the opportunity thus offered seems to have been accepted by worthy hands. Elizabeth Barry, to judge once more from the accounts of contemporaries, must have proved no undistinguished companion to Betterton. Creator of many famous rôles from Otway's heroines to Congreve's Zara in *The Mourning Bride* and his Marwood in *The Way of the World*, her " Presence of elevated Dignity," extolled by Cibber, was the counterpart of his. She had a " Mien and Motion superb, and gracefully majestick ; her Voice full, clear, and strong, so that no Violence of Passion could be too much for her : And when Distress, or Tenderness possess'd her, she subsided into the most affecting Melody, and Softness. In the Art of exciting Pity, she had a Power beyond all the Actresses I have yet seen, or what your Imagination can conceive. . . . In Scenes of Anger, Defiance, or Resentment, while she was impetuous and terrible, she pour'd out the Sentiment with an enchanting Harmony."

Alongside this tragic queen, the Mrs. Siddons of her day, stood many other noted actresses, tragic and comic. Nell Gwyn, during her brief stage decade, created Dryden's jaunty heroines, Florimel in *Secret Love* and Jacintha in *An Evening's Love.*

Mrs. Mountfort, with her variety and vivacity, essayed slightly more robust rôles—a hoyden in *The Western Lass*, for example—alongside of polished ladies like Melantha in *Marriage à la Mode*. " Melantha," to quote Cibber again,

> is as finish'd an Impertinent, as ever flutter'd in a Drawing-Room, and seems to contain the most compleat System of Female Foppery, that could possibly be crowded into the tortured Form of a Fine Lady. Her Language, Dress, Motion, Manners, Soul, and Body, are in a continual Hurry to be something more, than is necessary, or commendable. And though I doubt it will be a vain Labour, to offer you a just Likeness of Mrs. Monfort's Action, yet the fantastick Impression is still so strong in my Memory, that I cannot help saying something, tho' fantastically, about it. The first ridiculous Airs that break from her, are, upon a Gallant, never seen before, who delivers her a Letter from her Father, recommending him to her good Graces, as an honourable Lover. Here now, one would think she might naturally shew a little of the Sexe's decent Reserve, tho' never so slightly cover'd ! No, Sir ; not a Tittle of it ; Modesty is the Virtue of a poor-soul'd Country Gentlewoman ; she is too much a Court Lady, to be under so vulgar a Confusion ; she reads the Letter, therefore, with a careless, dropping Lip, and an erected Brow, humming it hastily over, as if she were impatient

to outgo her Father's Commands, by making a compleat Conquest of him at once ; and that the Letter might not embarrass her Attack, crack ! she crumbles it at once into her Palm, and pours upon him her whole Artillery of Airs, Eyes, and Motion ; down goes her dainty, diving Body, to the Ground, as if she were sinking under the conscious Load of her own Attractions ; then launches into a Flood of fine Language, and Compliment, still playing her Chest forward in fifty Falls and Risings, like a Swan upon waving Water ; and, to complete her Impertinence, she is so rapidly fond of her own Wit, that she will not give her Lover Leave to praise it : Silent assenting Bows, and vain Endeavours to speak, are all the share of the Conversation he is admitted to, which, at last, he is relieved from, by her Engagement to half a Score Visits, which she *swims* from him to make, with a Promise to return in a Twinkling.

Cibber's description is invaluable as indicating the way in which Dryden's vivacious heroines adumbrated Congreve's Millamant ; and the way, too, in which a Mrs. Mountfort suggested the style which was to make famous an Ann Bracegirdle, " the Darling of the Theatre " in 1700, creator of that lively lady of fashion in *The Way of the World.* For Mrs. Bracegirdle " the most eminent Authors " wrote their favourite characters. " If anything," thought Cibber, could excuse that desperate Extravagance of Love, that almost frantick Passion of Lee's Alexander the Great, it must have been, when Mrs. Bracegirdle was his Statira : As when she acted Millamant, all the Faults, Follies, and Affectation of that agreeable Tyrant were venially melted down into so many Charms and Attractions of a conscious Beauty.

From Mrs. Mountfort to Mrs. Bracegirdle is but a step ; and but another step is it from this Millamant to Anne Oldfield, toast of the early eighteenth century and equally impertinent creator of affected ladies. Mrs. Oldfield simply carries a tradition into another age.

CHAPTER V

TRAFFICKINGS into France, when Betterton scoured the Parisian theatres in search of scenic novelties, machines brought from a neighbour nation—these meant that up to the end of the seventeenth century the English stage had kept well abreast of the Continent. Maybe London had no wonder-working Giacomo Torelli, who awed his spectators by the marvels of his machinery, but it had competent workmen, and at least one architectural master, Sir Christopher Wren, applied himself to the designing of theatres. It was so, too, with the drama. Under the leadership of Shakespeare a magnificent group of dramatists had brought the writing of plays far above the reach of other countries in that age. Even in the Restoration period this spirit of questing and of inventive creation had not died out, and the exponents of the comedy of manners deserve an honourable place alongside Molière.

Immediately after this date, however, a kind of lethargy seems to fall upon the London stage. Addison's *Cato* in 1713 marked the last, the very last, of anything approaching tragic temper, and although, even after Congreve's *The Way of the*

World, produced in 1700, seemed to give a brilliant final flourish to the witty comedy of manners, a number of comic playwrights still continued to keep alive something of the old spirit, the glories of seventeenth-century comedy had gone.   So, too, the theatre languished.   In so far as theatre structure and scenic design are concerned nothing was produced in any way comparable to the magnificent work undertaken by the masters of Italy.   Inigo Jones deserves an esteem equal to that accorded to Buontalenti and Parigi, but no theatre-workers of the later age challenge the position occupied by the Bibienas or even that assumed by the many other, lesser-known perhaps but often brilliant, scene designers and architects who carried their ideals throughout the length and breadth of Europe.   In London, it is to be feared, little was to be seen in ordinary plays save eternal repetitions of uninteresting side wings and imitative back-cloths.   When Christopher Rich abandoned, or rather was driven from, Drury Lane in 1709, *The Tatler* made sport of his scenery and properties :

> This is to give Notice, that a magnificent Palace, with great Variety of Gardens, Statues, and Water-works, may be bought cheap in Drury Lane, where there are likewise several Castles to be disposed of, very delightfully situated ; as also Groves, Woods, Forrests, Fountains, and Country Seats, with very pleasant Prospects on all Sides of them, being the Moveables of

Ch——r R——ch, Esq., who is breaking up
Housekeeping, and has many curious Pieces
of Furniture to dispose of which may be seen
between the Hours of Six and Ten in the
Evening.

INVENTORY :

Spirits of Right Nantz Brandy, for Lambent
    Flames and Apparitions.
Three Bottles and a Half of Lightning.
One Shower of Snow in the whitest French
    Paper.
Two Showers of a browner Sort.
A Sea, consisting of a Dozen large Waves ; the
    Tenth bigger than ordinary, and a little
    damaged.
A dozen and a half of Clouds, trimmed with
    black, and well-conditioned.
A Rainbow, a little faded.
A Set of Clouds after the French Mode, streaked
    with Lightning, and furbelowed.
A new Moon something decay'd . . .
A Coach very finely gilt, and little used, with
    a Pair of Dragons, to be sold cheap.
A Setting Sun, a Pennyworth.
An Imperial Mantle made for Cyrus the Great,
    and worn by Julius Cæsar, Bajazet, King
    Henry the Eighth, and Signor Valentini.
A Basket-Hilt Sword, very convenient to carry
    Milk in.
Roxana's Night-Gown.
Othello's Handkerchief . . .

A Wild Boar kill'd by Mrs. Tofts and Dioclesian.

A Serpent to sting Cleopatra.

A Mustard-Bowl to make Thunder with,

Another of a bigger Sort, by Mr. D[enn]is's Directions, little used . . .

The Whiskers of a Turkish Bassa.

The Complexion of a Murderer in a Band-box ; consisting of a large Piece of burnt Cork, and a Coal-black Peruke.

A Suit of Clothes for a Ghost, *viz.* a bloody Shirt, a Doublet curiously pink'd, and a Coat with three great Eyelet-Holes upon the Breast . . .

Modern Plots, commonly known by the Name of Trap-Doors, Ladders of Ropes, Visard-Masques, and Tables with broad Carpets over them . . .

A Plume of Feathers, never used but by Œdipus and the Earl of Essex.

Satirical though the intent of this list may be, it assuredly errs not over far from the truth. Just such a litter of " decayed " and trumpery properties must have been in the possession of Drury Lane in 1709.

None the less, the stage of the eighteenth century deserves attention for various reasons. First, because it is during this period that we can trace the gradual approach made toward the theatre of to-day. Throughout the course of these years the conventions were being formed which, modified in various ways, have become the familiar conventions of the twentieth-century stage—the stage, too, not only of London but of New York as well. Here enters in the second element of interest in the eighteenth-century playhouse, its influence on America. From the time when Tony Aston, about the year 1702, adventurously wandered out to the new colonies, a series of English actors crossed the Atlantic and established at Charleston, at Williamsburg, at New York, and at Boston a theatre kin to that which they had known in England. To appreciate the history of the American theatre demands an appreciation of the contemporary stage in London and the provinces. If, on the other hand, the eighteenth century was slowly building up the playhouse of to-day, we must recognize that in it may be discovered the lingering of countless old traditions. In spite of continual change, the theatrical world from 1700 to 1780 was exceedingly traditional, so that for scholar and playgoer alike it has the interest of showing many of the conventions which ruled in Shakespeare's day, and of showing them more clearly because of a greater wealth of evidence. Considerable new light, for example, has been thrown on the subject of play-piracy on the part of dishonest Elizabethan publishers by Crompton Rhodes's investigation of similar methods of surreptitiously obtaining dramatic texts in the days of Sheridan. This example may serve to stand for many others affecting both the theatrical and dramatic conditions of the two periods.

Structurally but little alteration was made in the theatre itself. The old Theatre Royal in Drury Lane, periodically refurbished and partly rebuilt, continued in occupation until 1791. Lincoln's Inn Fields, taken over by Betterton's seceding actors in 1695 when the Union of the Companies (established in 1682) was broken, was used until 1705 ; and the *New Theatre* there, opened by John Rich in 1714, probably introduced no startling innovations. *Covent Garden*, opened in 1732, also by John Rich, assumed the mantle of Lincoln's Inn Fields and looked back to the original patent granted to D'Avenant in 1660. Altered in 1782 and enlarged in 1792, it endured until the disastrous fire of 1808.

One thing about theatre building in London during this period, however, must be noted. As we shall see, the playgoing public was rapidly increasing, and that increase is reflected in the numbers of new stages which established themselves in the metropolis. Designed by Sir John Vanbrugh, *The Queen's Theatre in the Haymarket* (known later variously as *The Opera House, The King's Theatre*, or simply *The Haymarket*) appeared in 1705. Little used for plays, it became the home of the Italian opera, and here was the scene of Händel's chief activities. This being burned in 1789, a new King's Theatre was erected in 1790 ; that, as *Her Majesty's*, was also destroyed by fire in 1867. A second theatre in the Haymarket was commonly called *The Little Theatre*. Opened in 1720, it witnessed a remarkable success under the tenancy of Henry Fielding (1735–1737). Still a third Haymarket house, *The Theatre Royal*, was built in 1766 by Samuel Foote on the site of the former. It endured till 1825, when the present Theatre Royal took its place. Besides these were two theatres in *Goodman's Fields*, one opened by Giffard (1729) in Leman Street, and another, in Ayliffe Street, built in 1731. Here David Garrick made his first appearance in London. *Sadler's Wells* had a variety house by 1740 ; rebuilt in 1765, the theatre there had a chequered career, specializing in pantomimes and spectacular shows until Phelps made dramatic history by selecting it for his series of Shakespearian revivals. At Wellclose Square in Goodman's Fields John Palmer erected *The Royalty* in 1787. A home of musical variety, it became known as *The East London Theatre* in 1810, and was destroyed by fire in 1826. A short-lived opera house, *The Pantheon*, in Oxford Street, was built in 1790 and gutted in 1792 ; the portico still remains as the front of Gilbey's wine store.

The significance of this fairly active theatre building may be left for later discussion. Here we must consider the general arrangements for stage and auditorium in these various houses. Apart from the opera houses, which tended to assume Italianate features (particularly the arrangement of the galleries in rows of boxes), the playhouses of the time agreed in displaying common elements and in adopting modifications by general consent. The large apron of the Restoration

stage tended to become less deep, thus approaching
the modern form, and the four doors in front of
the proscenium arch were accordingly reduced to
two.   Colley Cibber describes the beginning of
this change at the Theatre Royal in Drury Lane,
and attributes it to the desire for additional seating
accommodation.   Since the passage includes an
interesting comment on the resultant changes in
performance, his words may be given in their
entirety :

It must be observ'd, then, that the Area, or
Platform of the old Stage, projected about
four Foot forwarder, in a Semi-oval Figure,
parallel to the Benches of the Pit ; and that the
former, lower Doors of Entrance for the Actors
were brought down between the two foremost
(and then only) Pilasters ; in the Place of which
Doors, now the two Stage-Boxes are fixt.
That where the Doors of Entrance now are,
there formerly stood two additional Side-Wings,
in front to a full Set of Scenes, which had then
almost a double Effect, in their Loftiness and
Magnificence.
By the Original Form, the usual Station of
the Actors, in almost every Scene, was advanc'd
at least ten foot nearer to the Audience, than
they now can be ; because, not only from the
Stage's being shorten'd, in front, but likewise
from the additional Interposition of those Stage-
Boxes, the Actors (in respect to the Spectators,
that fill them) are kept so much more back-

ward from the main Audience, than they us'd
to be : But when the Actors were in Possession
of that forwarder Space, to advance upon, the
Voice was then more in the Centre of the House,
so that the most distant Ear had scarce the least
Doubt, or Difficulty in hearing what fell from
the weakest Utterance : All Objects were thus
drawn nearer to the Sense ; every painted Scene
was stronger ; every grand Scene and Dance
more extended ; every rich, or fine-coloured
Habit had a more lively Lustre : Nor was the
minutest Motion of a Feature (properly changing with the Passion, or Humor it suited) ever
lost, as they frequently must be in the Ob-
scurity of too great a Distance : And how
valuable an Advantage the Facility of hearing
distinctly, is to every well-acted Scene, every
common Spectator is a Judge.

Cibber's complaints, of course, have to be interpreted in the (literal) light of his theatre,
when candles and oil-lamps might readily render
" obscure " any objects far removed from sight.
Those complaints, however, were of no avail ;
the apron definitely became smaller as decades
advanced.

Otherwise, the playhouses of the time maintained the shape and arrangement which had been
theirs in the Restoration. Pit, box, and gallery
served for the auditorium ; stage and apron were
still used by the players. True, for the most part
the houses were larger ; in this age came the vogue

of the enormous playhouse which, although it did not reach full proportions until the very end of the century, is to be traced back to the earlier years. Partly due to the increasing body of spectators, the movement is also to be associated with the introduction of spectacle—a frequently satirized element between 1700 and 1800.

The cause of its success then was due to two things. One was the vogue of pantomime and the other was the rise of the " minor " unlicensed playhouse. Pantomime, as we know it, ultimately takes its rise from the Italian *commedia dell'arte* with its stock theatrical types—Pantalone and Dottore, Arlecchino and Brighella, Colombina and Nespola. Back in the sixteenth century the Italian players had been known in England ; Shakespeare himself, as recent research has demonstrated, did not disdain to borrow from their productions. With the return of Charles II. several of their troupes visited London, the chief among them being that captained by Tiberio Fiorillo, famous as Scaramuccia (Scaramouch). These definitely influenced a number of English playwrights, and certainly contributed something to the styles of histrionic interpretation of comic characters during this period. In the early decades of the eighteenth century further companies of French and Italian actors came to perform in London theatres, making such appeal that portions of their repertory, in adapted forms, began to intrude into the repertoires of Drury Lane itself. That they intruded so was largely due to the custom of

providing entr'acte entertainments and of performing a farce alongside of a regular five-act
tragedy or comedy. At first these entr'acte entertainments were almost entirely confined to the
occasional appearance of opera-singers, acrobats,
and dancers. Exhibitions of skill on the tight-rope
" with a child standing upright on " the shoulders
of some Madame Violante, " an Italian lady cele-
brated for her Strength and Agility " (" a Quali-
fication," as a contemporary commented, " that
does not render the Fair Sex the least more
amiable "), with swords, too, " tied to her legs
and two children to her feet "—these captured
public attention and were sure of drawing crowds.

It was at Lincoln's Inn Fields that the English
pantomime was born. Early in the century had
arisen a special kind of mimic show, invented by
John Weaver, who thought that with this he was
establishing on the modern stage an entertainment
kin to the " mimes and pantomimes " of ancient
Rome. This Weaver sort of pantomime consisted
usually of a classical legend expressed mainly
through ballet action, with the introduction of a
few operatic arias and a spice of comic business.
Popularity was accorded its inception, and soon,
owing to the success of the Italian troupes, it
gathered to itself elements familiar in the *commedia
dell'arte* shows. By 1727 " Harlequin is the only
Wit in Vogue " ; every theatre was engaged in
producing pieces of the kind. Of English Harle-
quins one man, by his mimetic skill and acrobatic
agility, proved himself the chief. This was John

Rich (or, as he styled himself, John Lun), of Lincoln's Inn Fields. Unhappily, he had one great defect—he could not express himself so ably through words as he could through actions. The result was that, the better to exploit his own talents, he introduced and popularized a special type of wordless pantomime. This, meeting with the former, gave rise to a pantomime performance in which arias were given to certain characters, whilst the more comic persons, such as Harlequin, carried on their stories in dumb-show. Dumb show necessarily demanded rich and spectacular effects, and since the pantomime proved more popular than the literary drama, the managers of the two patent theatres found themselves forced to follow the lead set at the " minor " playhouses, and proceeded to vie with one another in the production of ever more and more ornate shows on these lines.

Not, however, without heartburning and at times faring poorly beside the livelier " minor houses." In the year 1724, when Cibber, Barton Booth, and Robert Wilks were joint managers of Drury Lane with Sir Richard Steele as nominal patentee, things came to a sorry pass. " Our audiences," wrote the managers to Steele,

> decrease daily, and these low entertainments, which you and we so heartily despise, draw the numbers, whilst we act only to the few who are blest with common sense. Though the opera is worn, yet it draws better than before,

and some persons of distinction have engaged
French comedians to come over to the Haymarket. Thus, while there are three playhouses
exhibiting nonsense of different kinds against
us, it is impossible we should subsist much
longer. Both the Courts have forsaken us.
All we can do is to make the best of a losing
game, and part from the whole on the best
terms we can. No person living but ourselves
is sensible of the low state we are reduced to,
therefore we need not observe to you how very
needful it is to keep the secret. . . . Our profits
were ever more than double to what they have
been this year, and we are very far from any
hopes of their growing better.

This melancholy epistle reads as if it had been
indited by some modern theatre-lover complain-
ing of the cinema's encroaching power ; and
maybe we shall not be far wrong in likening the
development of pantomimic spectacle and of
minor theatres to that of the film and the
" picture houses " of to-day.

Satirically, the author of *The Touch-Stone* (1728)
turned on the managers, ironically accusing them
of " prodigious Oeconomy in the Decorations of
the Stage " :

It is morally impossible for any POET, or
Master of a Play-House, to be too expensive in
the Beauty or Grandeur of their SCENES and
MACHINES : The more just and surprizing they

appear, the sooner will the Spectator be led insensibly into imagining every thing real, and, of consequence, prove the easier perswaded of the Instruction intended: Besides, they are absolutely necessary in all Parts of a PLAY, where the Plot requires the Intervention of some supernatural Power, in order to conquer Difficulties, and solve Misteries: For, what is a God, or a Devil, or a Conjurer,—without Moving Clouds, Blazing Chariots, Flying Dragons, and Enchanted Castles?—Airy Sprites, Terrestrial Hob-goblins, and Infernal Demons, must, at a Word, descend, rise, and vanish. These things, justly introduc'd, strike an Awe upon the Audience; and, while they are amaz'd and delighted, they are instructed. This gives the STAGE a Character with the World, and POETS and ACTORS are esteem'd Demi-gods. Thus, when People are pre-possess'd in Favour of their Power, they dare not but embrace their Doctrines. . . .

The Habits of the Actors likewise have a prodigious Influence on the Minds of an Audience. We see daily, in the great World, a vast Deference shewn to the figure of a Suit of Cloaths; and how regularly Degrees of Respect rise, from the Gold and Silver Button and Button-hole, to Lace and Embroidery. How nicely are the Distances betwixt Cloth, Velvet, and Brocade, observ'd? Much more in the THEATRE should this Distinction prevail, where our Senses are to be touch'd, pleas'd, and taken by Surprize; and where every Spectator, indeed, is to receive an Impression of the Character of the Person from his Dress; and the first Ideas are generally most lasting.

TRAGEDY borrows vast Advantages from the additional Ornaments of Feathers and high Heels; and it is impossible, but that two Foot and a Half of Plume and Buskin must go a great Length in giving an Audience a just Notion of a Hero. . . .

The Appearance of a Retinue suitable to every distinct Character of the Drama, (which should make a Figure on the Stage) is another Point of very great Consequence, and ought to be principally regarded. What is a Tyrant without his Guards? or a Princess, without her Maids of Honour? A General, without a Troop of Officers? Or, a first Minister, without a Levee of Spies and Dependants? A Lawyer, without a Flock of Clients? Or, a Beau, without a Train of Lacquies?

This tendency towards the elaboration of spectacular effects received impetus even from that which at first sight would have seemed to imply the destruction of its fosterers, the " minor " theatres. Theoretically, of course, Drury Lane and Covent Garden alone had the right to present dramatic entertainments, but circumstances, particularly the growth of the playgoing public, proved so strong that the exacter terms of the patents were ignored, and at the time when

The Beggar's Opera was produced and when Henry Fielding, the future novelist, managed his own troupe of comedians, these " minors " had assumed a position of prime importance. Maybe they would have been permitted to continue their careers unchecked had not Fielding himself unwittingly contributed to their temporary downfall. Witty and satirical, he started to write and produce a series of mordant burlesques. Some of these would have passed, being, like *Tom Thumb*, directed only at the follies of the stage ; but from literary satire Fielding turned to political and attacked the vices of the ministry. *The Author's Farce* was followed by *Pasquin*, and that by *The Historical Register*. The Prime Minister, Walpole, grew worried, and at length determined to cut out this irritating thorn in the government's side. By some chicanery he received parliamentary support for his famous Licensing Act of 1737, and with it the freedom of the minor theatres temporarily vanished.

Vanished, at least, in theory. The purpose of the new bill was, first, to restrict the performance of drama to the two patent houses, and, second, to control the playwrights by the imposition of a clearly defined censorship. In practice, however, the already moderately powerful " minor " theatres found ways of escape. One such consisted in advertising a concert or a " tea," for which fairly high prices were charged, and at which (" gratis ") a rehearsal of a play was presented. By this means any drama might be

given performance unlicensed. Another, and
more important, development was that which
eventually led to the establishment of the nineteenth century "burletta." If the minor playhouses were forbidden openly to make charge for
the presentation of tragedy and comedy, they
could, and did, provide ever-increasing audiences
with spectacular pieces, generally of a wordless
kind. Various houses of the type erected at
Sadler's Wells specialized in this form of entertainment, and obviously drew spectators away from
the major theatres. In vying with the greater
managers the "minors," finding that spectacle was
desired, exploited spectacle for all they were worth.
Spending enormous sums of money for a single
production, they tended ever more and more to
keep one show in constant performance for considerable periods, with the result that they virtually
established the rule of the modern "run." The
major theatres had to struggle hard to compete
with their enemies, whom they at once despised
and hated, and they found that those enemies
could be met, if not vanquished, only by the
adoption of greater and greater spectacle. Spectacle, however, costs money, and the comparatively
small theatres of earlier times soon had to make
way for those enlarged structures, already referred
to, which were calculated to bring higher receipts
to the managers. A vicious circle was set a-rolling,
for it was discovered that, the vastness of the new
theatres preventing those in the further parts of
the house from hearing ordinary spoken dialogue,

only the broadest of effects might now be introduced. From the operation of competitive effort
and from necessity alike spectacle increased and
pantomimic shows ruled the stage.

Spectacle, of course, itself demands considerable
means at the service of the manager, and it has
to be confessed that, if England possessed no
Bibiena, the theatres did progress in material
resources. The Restoration stage had established
firmly the convention of the back shutters and
side wings, and this convention endured for many
years—has, indeed, endured to our own times.
Alongside of this, on the other hand, we find many
theatrical developments, particularly in the latter
half of the eighteenth century. Built-up effects—
that is to say, simulated rocks and castles and
greenswards—often took the place of, or were used
along with, the side wings. The flats became less
flimsy and less patently artificial ; practicable
doors and windows frequently appeared in them.
Fire effects were often indulged in, and lighting
devices, such as the ." Eidophusikon," provided
thrills for an audience which had previously known
only the primitive and artificial clouds painted
upon flat strips of canvas.

The appearance of this " Eidophusikon " indicates the great advances which had been made in
lighting. Up to the time of Garrick, the methods
of illumination were primitive in the extreme.
The auditorium seems to have remained in brightness during the performance of every play, the
candles arranged at intervals along the edges of

Reproduced from " The Development of the Theatre " (Harrap).

ROMEO AND JULIET IN THE 18TH CENTURY.
From a print in the possession of
Mr. Herbert Norris.

the galleries being left to splutter from the time
that the curtain was raised to the closing of the
theatre.

For the stage itself there were three main sources
of illumination. The chief of these was the rings
or " hoops " of candles suspended from the roof
over the apron or the stage. Not shaded in any
way, the candles burned in full view of the
audience, providing what, we must imagine, was
an eye-aching glare. By the sides of the proscenium were also set wall brackets, but the few
candles there furnished apparently little additional
light. More important were the " floats " or
footlights—a series of candles or lamps placed
originally without a shield along the front of the
apron, and later concealed by a bar of wood or
placed in a trough. Footlights, be it noted, were
no modern invention. They are clearly seen in
the " Red Bull " engraving of 1673, and we find
them referred to nearly a century earlier in Italian
writings. Although references to them are scant,
we are forced to believe that they formed a regular
part of the lighting equipment of every post-
Restoration English playhouse.

These conditions endured until the year 1765,
when Garrick, after a visit to the Continent, returned full of enthusiasm in the possession of an
idea for a complete reorganizing of the theatre's
illumination. First of all, he obtained a set of
new lamps. " I have carried out your two com-
missions," he heard from Jean Monnet, director
of the Opéra Comique,

and with M. Boquet's designs I will send you a
reflector and two different samples of the lamp
you want for the footlights at your theatre.
There are two kinds of reflectors : those that
are placed in a niche in the wall, and which
have one wick ; and those which are hung up
like a chandelier, and have five. . . . As to the
lamps for lighting your stage, they are of two
kinds : some are of earthenware, and in biscuit
form ; they have six or eight wicks, and you
put oil in them ; the others are of tin, in the
shape of a candle, with a spring, and you put
candles in them.

Further information followed in another letter
concerning torches in which licopodium might be
burned. That Garrick's introduction of new
instruments was of importance may not be denied,
but of far greater significance was his almost
complete rearrangement of these and earlier
instruments. Briefly, this seems to have consisted
in the banishing of the rings and the placing of
candles or lamps either behind the side wings or
at least behind suitable shades. In itself, the
change does not appear so epoch-making, yet
Garrick's innovation was revolutionary in its
results. It meant that now the portion of the
stage behind the proscenium arch was more
brightly illuminated than the apron, consequently
the actors tended to move back from the audience, and the already curtailed apron lost even
such significance as it still retained. It meant,

too, that no row of lights prevented those in the galleries from seeing the rear of the stage, so that processions and the like might more freely be exploited. And above all, it meant that the basis was now provided for more elaborate, more easily controlled, more pleasing, and more realistic effects. The path was being opened up which the theatre was to tread in the following century.

The exploitation of pantomime and spectacle which characterizes the playhouses of this age must ultimately be traced back to the audiences who frequented the theatres and induced the managers to pursue these methods. Vastly unlike were the spectators of 1720 from those of 1670. Perhaps the former might still indulge in riot and clamour ; perhaps they might still maintain a buzz of conversation during the performance of plays ; but their riot and their conversation were at once more decorous and less gracefully artistic than those which had brightened Restoration playhouses. The courtiers of Charles II. were thoroughly disreputable, but they had wit and grace and a true feeling for art. Many of the spectators in an eighteenth-century theatre were dully bourgeois and dismally moral in their out-look upon life. A change had come over society. In 1698 Jeremy Collier issued his sensational attack on the profaneness and immorality of the English stage, and his work but expressed in more violent terms what many folk had been thinking since the death of Charles II. We must not be surprised, therefore, to find, within a year or two of the last excesses of Buckingham and Rochester, almost in the very midst of the flowering comedy of manners, a London aristocracy which patronized Societies for the Reformation of Manners. The Court led the way. Queen Anne strove to be decorously polite, and her satellites followed her intentions even if at times they succeeded only in being vulgarly vicious. Art, one has to confess, generally flourishes most in periods of moral freedom, and the restraint of eighteenth-century existence, even if it was only outward, did something to kill that spirit which had sparkled joyously and hilariously and improperly in earlier times.

This altered tone among the aristocracy was increased by a movement within society itself. The middle classes, who had been derided in the days of Charles, gradually edged themselves into the hitherto exclusive circles, and the theatres, as a consequence, had to provide for an audience no longer almost exclusively of the Court, but representing both the aristocracy and the upper middle classes.

As years went by, the number of middle-class spectators grew, until even two greatly enlarged theatres with several minor houses proved insufficient to cater for the needs of the public. This growth of the public led to altered conditions for the actors and the managers. It meant that, instead of catering for a small and select class, they had to think of larger audiences in which the less refined and the less witty preponderated ; it meant that " hornpipes and dances " had to be freely introduced in order to please the more vulgar tastes, that sensibility had to colour most works in order to satisfy middle-class prejudices, and that such occasional touches of wit as were provided for the last remnants of the polished aristocracy had to be veiled and confined until they lost their point and savour. The eighteenth-century theatre is essentially a theatre of the upper-middle class, and, in its lack of true harmony in proportion, in its medley of diverse elements inartistically strung together, it is typical of that class's taste.

The age, however, did not want for great actors. The century opened with two theatres in which were gathered artists of no mean distinction, and their brilliance was reflected by many others in the succeeding years. Colley Cibber in foppish parts, Doggett as the low comedy man, and Mrs. Oldfield as the pert lady of fashion must have provided a trio such as might rarely be found in any one generation. The vitality of the performers is to be traced in the development of acting styles, for histrionic art did not by any means remain static during these hundred years. Writing in 1830 John Bernard cast a long glance over his memories of the theatre and stated that

there have been four distinguishable schools on the London stage, since its restoration under Charles II. The first, that of Betterton, who modelled, in some measure, on the French taste ; the next, Booth, Wilks, and Cibber's (in which Digges and Quin, Mossop, Sheridan, and Barry, were instructed); thirdly, Garrick's; fourthly (which is the present), John Kemble's.

A survey of extant information from contemporary sources indicates that this résumé does not fall far short of the truth. Betterton's rhetorical and bombastic style, although based as much on earlier English example as on the French, must have borne a fairly close resemblance to that familiar in Parisian theatres at the end of the seventeenth century. When he, in Pepys' words, " did the prince's part [Hamlet] beyond imagination," we may believe that he infused into it something at least of contemporary " heroic " quality. The group of early eighteenth-century players whom Bernard mentions—Cibber, Booth, Wilks—while they owed much to Betterton's example, clearly were evolving a method distinct from his. The difference is that between the fierce outbursts of heroic rhodomontade in the rimed plays of 1670 and the more staidly dignified accents of Addison's *Cato*. The first still preserves something of earlier Elizabethan abandon, the passion of an Alleyn ; the second is coloured by the intellectual, rationalistic tendencies of a pseudo-classic and " Augustan " society. The style of Cibber, excelling in would-be fops and those who aped the manners of fine gentlemen, is thoroughly typical ; Barton Booth had just the right interpretation for the duller tragedy of the eighteenth century ; and Robert Wilks, with his sprightly air in comedy and more subdued treatment of tragedy, was obviously their true companion.

Wilks, "erect, and of a pleasing Aspect," indefatigable in his labours and so exact that Cibber questioned " if in forty Years, he ever five times chang'd or misplac'd an Article " in any one of his parts, stands forward representative of the gentlemen who read and appreciated *The Spectator*, who found their poetic expression in the work of Pope. " He was justly admired as an actor," remarks Davies, " and loved as an honest man ; but had no mark to discriminate him from any other private gentleman." Booth had a stronger, a more powerful and at the same time a more mannered interpretation. Characteristically, his greatest success came in *Cato*, wherein he discovered just such a part as suited his genius. " He had the Deportment of a Nobleman, and so well became a Star and Garter, he seemed born to it." Without mouthing or ranting, he yet bestowed a monumental tone upon all rôles he assumed ; not without significance is the fact that, having " a good Taste for Statuary and Painting . . . these he frequently studied, and sometimes borrowed Attitudes from." One particular quality he possessed —" he could soften and slide over, with a kind of elegant Negligence, the Improprieties in a Part he acted, while, on the contrary, he would dwell with Energy upon the Beauties, as if he exerted a latent Spirit which had been kept back for such an Occasion, that he might alarm, awaken, and transport in those Places only, where the Dignity

of his own góod Sense could be supported by
that of his Author." Precisely this was needed
by Augustan tragedy, and we can imagine in
Booth's hands the stiffly conventional heroes receiving an interpretation, harmonious in its quality,
bringing out to the full those elements of strength
and dignified sense which was all the age could
provide in this kind.

Garrick's innovation, about the year 1750, consisted in a more determined approach towards
reality, and in so far his method of interpretation
bears a distinct relationship to the growing power
of proto-romantic sentiment which is so marked
a feature of the literary work during his time. In
assessing Garrick's position we must remember
that " the noble warmth, masterly elocution, and
graceful action of Booth " together with " the
animated spirit, elegant address, and fine feelings
of Wilks " had declined into mannerisms, and that
the stage was in the possession of men decidedly
weaker than their predecessors. Ryan was but
a " useful " performer at the best, yet to him fell
many of the rôles made distinguished by Wilks.
Bridgewater, too, " was esteemed a general player,"
but " it was with some a doubt whether he acted
best or worst in tragedy or comedy." Milward
and Delane were passable lovers, Quin an un-
inspiring exponent of tragic heroes. Garrick
infused something new into an art that had become
traditional and unadventuresome. He approached
his parts emotionally and from a fresh angle,
instead of intellectually and from the point of

view of the past. Whereas other players had copied from this earlier master or that, Garrick created his own versions. Thus, for example, Theophilus Cibber had made a success in Abel Drugger (of Jonson's *The Alchemist*); and the general tendency would have been to model a further interpretation upon what Cibber had already done. Such, however, was not Garrick's way. His

> Abel Drugger was of a different species from Cibber's. The moment he came upon the stage, he discovered such awkward simplicity, and his looks so happily bespoke the ignorant, selfish, and absurd tobacco merchant, that it was a contest not easily to be decided, whether the burst of laughter or applause were loudest. Through the whole part he strictly preserved the modesty of nature.

The same he did in his creation of tragic parts. That for which he was praised—" his preserving consistency of character "—proved merely the result of a general endeavour to approach his subjects in a manner at once original and in conformity with what he had observed in life.

This fresh approach, with its insistence upon the real world, requires careful consideration. No doubt, were we to be granted a sight of Garrick now, he might seem cold and artificial to us who are familiar with such diverse later styles, but for his age his acting was almost naturalistic in its abandonment of convention. To this there is Fielding's testimony. In *Tom Jones* Partridge goes to see *Hamlet*. He is all contemptuous of the Ghost until Garrick enters ; then he

> fell into such a violent fit of trembling that his knees knocked against each other. Jones asked him what was the matter, and whether he was afraid of the warrior upon the stage ? "O la, sir," said he, "I perceive now it is what you told me. I am not afraid of anything ; for I know it is but a play. And if it really was a ghost, it could do one no harm at such a distance, and in so much company ; and yet if I was frightened, I am not the only person." "Why, who," cries Jones, "doth thou take to be such a coward here besides thyself ? " "Nay, you may call me a coward if you will ; but if that little man there upon the stage is not frightened, I never saw any man frightened in my life.

At the conclusion of the performance Partridge is asked which actor he liked best, and unhesitatingly chooses the King ; and, on being told that the town's approval went unanimously to Hamlet, he ejaculates :

> "He the best player ! . . . why, I could act as well as he myself. I am sure if I had seen a ghost, I should have looked in the very same manner and done just as he did. And then, to

be sure, in that scene, as you called it, between him and his mother, where you told me he acted so fine, why, Lord help me, any man, that is, any good man, that had such a mother would have done exactly the same. I know you are only joking with me ; but, indeed, madam, though I was never at a play in London, yet I have seen acting before in the country, and the King for my money : he speaks all his words distinctly, half as loud again as the other. Anybody may see he is an actor.

The twirling of the handkerchief at the end of the play-scene, the kicking down of the chair on the ghost's reappearance—business of this sort was entirely in tune with the general spirit of his acting. Garrick, however, was not really the creator of a school ; in his extraordinary success and popularity he remained solitary. His achieve-ment was a kind of *tour de force*, and a testimony rather to his own individual genius than to a definite change of taste in his period.

The intellectual style, therefore, proceeded on its career even when he had indicated fresh ways of theatrical approach. Mrs. Siddons and John Kemble were, like Booth and Wilks, " classical " actors, the only difference being that, touched by the spirit of their age, they endeavoured to intro-duce at least something of fire into their portrayals, and borrowed directly from Greece a glimpse of added grandeur. Where Betterton and Booth still bore the arms of France on their crests,

Mrs. Siddons aimed at the creation of a grand style entirely independent of anything to be seen in the Parisian playhouses. Where Betterton is the companion of Dryden and Booth that of Pope, she, with her majestic sense of power, finds kinship among the rising Coleridges and Wordsworths of 1800. " In Roman parts, and in the Roman costume," Kemble " seemed to the manner born;" these set him at ease and "there art seemed less, nature more." Of like kind was the art of Mrs. Siddons. A contemporary wrote of the impression created by her acting in the last years of the century, praising her dignity and grandeur :

Nor has nature been partially bountiful—she has endowed her with a quickness of conception, and a strength of understanding equal to the proper use of such extraordinary gifts. So entirely is she mistress of herself, so collected, and so determined in gestures, tone, and manner, that she seldom errs, like other actors, because she doubts her powers or comprehension. She studies her author attentively, conceives justly, and describes with a firm consciousness of propriety. She is sparing in her action, but it is always proper, picturesque, graceful, and dignified ; it arises immediately from the sentiments and feeling, and is not seen to prepare itself before it begins. No studied trick or start can be predicted ; no forced tremulation of the figure, where the vacancy of the eye declares the absence of passion, can be seen ; no laborious

strainings at false climax, in which the tired
voice reiterates one high tone beyond which
it cannot reach, is ever heard ; no artificial
heaving of the breasts, so disgusting when the
affectation is perceptible ; none of those arts
by which the actress is seen, and not the
character, can be found in Mrs. Siddons.
So natural are her gradations and transitions,
so classical and correct her speech and deportment, and so intensely interesting her voice,
form, and features, that there is no conveying
an idea of the pleasure she communicates by
words.

The emphasis here on grace, dignity, statuesque
proportions, testifies to the classical nature of her
art.

In enumerating these names, we must not, of
course, forget that the century was illuminated as
well by a host of players who, if not so universally
known as Garrick, each possessed his or her share
of talent.   Charles Macklin was one of these,
remembered because he revolutionized the treatment of Shylock by presenting that character as
an almost tragic villain.   Gay William Lewis interpreted well the comic gentlemen of late eighteenth-
century drama, and John Henderson won fame
for his Falstaff and his Hamlet.   Nor were the
actresses less skilful.   Vivacious Kitty Clive per-
sonated dozens of pert chambermaids and extra-
vagant ladies of fashion ; Peg Woffington was
popular for her comedy rôles ; and Mrs. Pritchard

by many was regarded as a rival in art to Mrs. Siddons.

Often has it been asserted that the very presence of these brilliant players was responsible for the weakness of eighteenth-century comedy and tragedy, but the basic cause of that weakness— which, perhaps, has been a trifle over-emphasized —is to be sought for, not among the actors, but among the spectators of the period. " The drama's laws the drama's patrons give " is a Johnsonian precept so frequently quoted as to have become trite ; but should we desire the most fitting example to prove its truth, to the eighteenth century we should go.

CHAPTER VI

TECHNICALLY, the theatre advanced from 1800 to 1900 at a pace far outstripping that marking stage development at any other period save perhaps the age of the Renaissance. Until the early decades of this century the traditional architectural form definitely established in the sixteen sixties had remained, and actors still appeared on the forward apron and generally preferred to make their exits by the proscenium doors, with a rimed tag on their lips and in their eyes a backward glance at the galleries. Already in 1767 some critics had recognized that the old apron was an unnecessary convention, observing that

> the actors, instead of being so brought forwards, ought to be thrown back at a certain distance from the spectator's eye, and stand within the scenery of the stage, in order to make a part of that pleasing illusion for which all dramatic exhibitions are calculated.

Convention, however, at that time proved too strong, and the apron remained. True, Drury Lane led the way in 1780 by banishing the doors and substituting therefor a pair of stage-boxes, but it would seem (although the evidence is somewhat contradictory) that these were restored at the instance of the actors, who felt " embarrassed by the more extended area of the stage," and the necessity each had of edging " away in his retreat towards the far distant wings." With Garrick's new system of lighting, on the other hand, the players themselves must have begun to observe that the further back they stood the more they were illuminated, since most of the stage lamps were now set, not in full sight of the audience at the sides or beneath the arch, but behind the scenery and the proscenium pillars. The result was a keen battle between theatrical conservatism and practical necessity, the latter winning a hard-fought struggle in the early years of the nineteenth century. In the famous *Rejected Addresses* of 1812 the ghost of Dr. Johnson is made to rise through a trap and comment upon the change :

Permanent stage doors we have none. That which is permanent cannot be removed ; for, if removed, it soon ceases to be permanent. What stationary absurdity can vie with that ligneous barricade which, decorated with frappant and tintinnabulant appendages, now serves as the entrance of the lowly cottage, and now as the exit of a lady's chamber. . . . To elude this glaring absurdity, to give to each respective mansion the door which the carpenter would

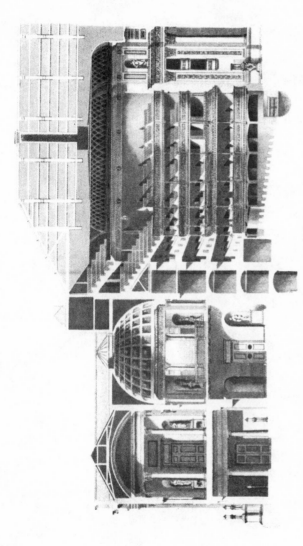

Section of Drury Lane Theatre (1812).
Architect, Benjamin Wyatt.

doubtless have given, we vary our portal with
the varying scene, passing from deal to mahogany, and from mahogany to oak, as the
opposite claims of cottage, palace, or castle
may appear to require.

Even at this time, however, the actors were loud
in their complaints, and to these this shade of
Johnson makes reference :

> The children of Thespis are general in their
> censures of the architect in having placed
> the locality of exit at such a distance from the
> oily radiators which now dazzle the eyes of
> him who addresses you. I am, cries the Queen
> of Terrors, robbed of my fair proportions.
> When the King-killing thane hints to the breath-
> less auditory the murders he means to perpe-
> trate in the castle of Macduff " ere my purpose
> cool," so vast is the interval he has to travel
> before he can escape from the stage, that his
> purpose has even time to freeze.

The complaints, indeed, were so numerous that
once more the doors were set back in place, not to
be " permanently " removed until the year 1822,
when the audience was bidden not to blame the
architect
> for transporting from the floors
> Those old offenders here—the two stage doors ;
> Doors which have oft with burnish'd panels
>   stood
> And golden knockers glittering in a wood,

> Which on their posts, through every change remain'd
>   Fast as Bray's Vicar, whosoever reign'd ;
> That served for palace, cottage, street or hall,
> Used for each place, and out of place in all ;
> Station'd, like watchmen who in lamplight sit,
> For all their business of the night unfit.

While it took many decades before the provincial theatres and even many playhouses in London itself fell into line, we may say that about this period, the twenties of the nineteenth century, the familiar modern picture-frame stage was established.

This picture-frame stage found new means at its command. Gas was commercially introduced in this time, and, evil-smelling though it might be, it obviously provided an illuminant far superior for theatrical purposes to what candles and oil-lamps ever could have been. Introduced first for the lighting of the exterior and foyers, then for the auditorium, and later for the stage, it offered opportunities which took years to realize. With the old methods there might be only the crudest kind of control. The footlights might be made to rise and sink ; silks might be employed as colour mediums for the behind-scene lamps ; and clumsy contrivances might be used to dim or darken the stage. But each lamp or candle remained a separate unit, and to attempt any kind of general transformation demanded the services of a whole army of attendants. Gas, so far as the stage was concerned, first provided theatre-workers with an illuminant which could be easily and effectively disciplined. Dimming now presented no difficulties ; and, with the gradual introduction of new inventions (such as limelight during the last years of Macready's management), various intensities and qualities of light were made immediately available. Perhaps the greatest revolution occasioned by the establishment of gas-lighting, however, was that which affected the auditorium. When Covent Garden in 1817 set up " a magnificent chandelier, which from the Centre of the Ceiling diffuses a soft and brilliant Light around, without obstructing the view of a single Spectator," a means had been given for the darkening of the house during the performance of the play. No longer was it necessary to have the auditorium fully illuminated, for the turn of a handle might lower the flaring jets. What this meant for the development of scene design and of " stage pictures " may readily be realized.

Invention did not stop at providing new lighting for the playhouses. Mechanical devices which would have gladdened the heart of Giacomo Torelli, famous machinist at Paris during the latter years of the seventeenth century, became common property, and the English stage, although before 1900 it possessed nothing so elaborate as Steele MacKaye introduced to New York audiences, rapidly improved its material resources. The new Drury Lane of 1812 had " accommodations for the stage . . . upon a much larger scale than those of any other theatre in Europe."

To facilitate the working of some scenery and light machinery, there is a stage about ten feet below the upper one, where the carpenters attend either to raise ghosts and pantomimic demons, or to obey the magic wand which consigns them to oblivion ; under this second stage there is a depth of about forty feet, furnished with various mechanical engines requisite for raising splendid and massy pillars, temples, etc., which enrich the scenery, and contribute so essentially to the effect produced by the grand ballets and pantomimes exhibited at this theatre.

In the roof of the theatre are contained, besides the barrel-loft, ample room for scene-painters, and four very large reservoirs, from which water is distributed over every part of the house, for the purpose of instantly extinguishing fire, in any part where such accident is possible.

Over the stage is a double range of galleries, called flies, containing machinery, and where the greatest part of the scenery is worked, but which, from the number of blocks, wheels, and ropes crossing each other in every direction, give it very much the appearance of a ship's deck.

The " large reservoirs " strike a modern note, as do the " forced ventilation " and the " Calorifere Fumivore Stoves" at Covent Garden in 1818, whereby " the Theatre can be either Cooled or Warmed, and the Atmosphere of the different

Dec. 25, 1858.

Victoria and Albert Museum.

THE INTERIOR OF THE NEW ADELPHI THEATRE, 1858.
ARCHITECT, T. H. WYATT.
(From the " Gabrielle Enthoven " Collection.)

Parts of the House can be kept to one pleasant Temperature throughout the different Seasons of the Year." In every way, both before and behind the curtain, the London playhouses during this time were assuming their present familiar features. " Stalls " shattered the unanimity of the old pit, and the system of reserving seats banished the fighting mobs described by Charles Lamb or the discreet footmen patiently holding " places." The cyclorama was tentatively experimented with ; Fechter divided his stage into sections ; Irving, making use of every means at his command, produced spectacular effects far beyond any pageantry known in earlier decades.

Much of this machinery tended, of course, to be employed for purposes not particularly worthy. In 1896 a commentator observed that " the thrill seems to be the popular thing among theatregoers nowadays," noting that " within the past decade the scene of a railway train of twelve coaches dashing madly through the darkness, to the accompaniment of the usual whistling, steam, and din," had made theatrical fortunes. This emphasis was but natural, for novelties, when first introduced, always tend to be exploited inartistically and for meretricious effect. But our concern is not with such employment of the new devices, more important being the service to which these were, or might be, put in the development of the more serious theatre. To discuss and appreciate that service demands a certain return to the eighteenth century, for this age inherited and brought to fulfilment many ideas and artistic styles which already had been adumbrated in the age of Garrick.

Every one knows that in literature the eighteenth century witnessed two great and largely antagonistic movements of the spirit. The one, associated with the name of Alexander Pope, is commonly called Augustanism, or Pseudo-Classicism ; the other, expressed most fully by the brilliant group of early nineteenth-century poets, is styled Romanticism. To define exactly the two terms is almost impossible. We may, however, say that the Augustan mind stood mainly for convention and rational acceptance of the immediately existent, while the romantic mind strove to escape from convention, and delighted, not only in the present, but in the exciting wonder of the past and in the glories of the purely visionary. Pope's world is mainly the world of fashionable London life ; Shelley's world embraces not only the Italy he loved, but the realms of antique Greece and the dream-fantasies which he conjured out of his own brain. The Augustans were dominated by the ideal of imitation in its narrower sense ; the romanticists ever strove towards something new, whether that something new was to be found in the past, in foreign realms, in imaginative visions, or in fields of human life untouched by contemporary society.

In tracing the development of this romantic movement in literature, two or three clearly marked tendencies are to be distinguished. There is the cult of the past, as exemplified variously in Percy's *Reliques of Ancient English Poetry*, Chatterton's *Rowley Poems*, the work of the historians, and Scott's novels. Besides this there is the belief in realism, expressed crudely by Crabbe and majestically by Wordsworth. The belief in realism has also one particular form, which may be described as a passion for the grand and the gloomy. The delight in graves seen in Young's *Night Thoughts* and in Gray's *Elegy* has something in common with Wordsworth's passion for the lofty mountains and dark tarns of a Cumberland landscape.

Obviously not all the qualities of romanticism are included in these three movements described above ; but these at least provide a great proportion of *motif* to the typical romantic poetry of the age, and it is precisely these qualities which are to be traced in the world of the theatre from about the middle of the eighteenth century. Up to 1750 scenic designers, except when engaged on some spectacular pantomime, rarely thought of anything but conventional palaces and prisons. Hardly ever did they endeavour to provide a proper historical setting for plays of the past, while the actors were content if some symbol appeared in their dress to indicate the station of life or the race they were supposed to be representing. *Othello, Antony and Cleopatra, King Lear*—all would be performed against a background of conventional baroque pillars and arches ; in the first the actor taking the title-rôle would wear a turban and a conventionally Eastern gown, with a scimitar at his side ; Antony would boast a semi-Roman breastplate ; while Lear would wear the ordinary clothes of the day, only half concealed by a flowing cloak trimmed with ermine to indicate his royalty. Early in the eighteenth century we begin to hear vague murmurs of dissatisfaction with these methods, and the true change in the theatre is heralded by the appearance of Macklin as Macbeth clad in what purported to be ancient Scots garments. Garrick followed with *Lear* in " ancient " British clothes, and from 1760 onwards we constantly meet with attempts on the part of one manager or another to secure historical accuracy. Historical accuracy of this kind was, of course, hopelessly inaccurate according to modern scholarly standards, and even contemporaries were frequently moved to ridicule. Macready's dress for Virginius, long after the new movement was under way, was " of the simplest, almost rudest kind—a pasteboard helmet covered with tin foil, a serge robe " and pasteboard gorgets, and for Hamlet

he wore a dress the waist of which nearly reached his arms ; a hat with a sable plume big enough to cover a hearse ; a pair of black silk gloves much too large for him ; a ballet shirt of straw-coloured satin, which looked simply dirty ; and, what with his gaunt, awkward, angular figure, his grizzled hair, his dark beard close shaven to his square jaws, yet unsoftened by a trace of pigment, his irregular features, his queer, extraordinary nose . . . and his long skinny neck, he appeared positively hideous.

From contemporary accounts, too, we realize that frequently the hero was clad in some kind of pretentious suit of " ancient " appearance, while his companions of lesser import wore the dress of the time. In Delap's *The Catives* (1786) Kemble thus sported Scots dress, but he was " the *only* one . . . that the parsimony of that day would consent to in the tragedy." If the entire cast was furnished with " historical " garments, these historical garments were put to many uses. Antony's Roman soldiers would be attired in the same armour as served for the forces of Henry V. at Agincourt. In 1805 Lord Harcourt, writing to Elliston, could honestly declare that

> our stage is still barbarous in respect of costume. A short waist, a modish head-dress, are often coupled in the old plays, with a Grecian robe and a Gothic ruff. I have seen Woodward and Dodd wear white satin heels to their shoes ; and Lewis, too, in such a dress as could only be fitting a mountebank in a fair.

One may note, too, that the actresses, afraid of seeming *outré*, refused for long to depart from the modishly correct. Mrs. Siddons seems to have been bolder than most, and maybe we may date a change in feminine theatrical wear to her tentative innovations about the turn of the century. " A little deferring to costume," she " relieved the

sable body and train of Lady Randolph by a great
deal of white covering upon her bosom, which
took with graceful propriety the form of the *ruff*.
And this was *much*, in those easy times, when
nobody thought of risking the *laughable* in the
CORRECT." She, too, was responsible for introducing the tendency towards statuesque simplicity
in attire when interpreting classical rôles. " The
actress," says Boaden, " had formerly complied
with fashion, and deemed the prevalent becoming ;
she now saw that tragedy was debased by the
flutter of light materials, and that the head, and
all its powerful action from the shoulder, should
never be encumbered by the monstrous inventions
of the hairdresser and the milliner."

Whatever inaccuracies there were, and however
slowly the fashion grew, the movement, flowing
slowly and with many eddies from 1760 to 1800,
gathered impetus in the early decades of the nineteenth century, and eventually swept like a torrent
over the whole stage. J. R. Planché's work in
procuring a new costuming of Shakespeare when
Charles Kemble presented his *King John* in 1823
was no real innovation in idea, whatever it might
have been in practice. What there was new in
this production was, first, the endeavour to make
all the characters conform to exactitude in dress,
and, secondly, the painstaking care with which
Planché himself set about the preparing of· his
sketches. He consulted Sir Samuel Meyrick,
authority on ancient armour, and pored over the
illuminated manuscripts which Douce lent him.

Victoria and Albert Museum.

CHARLES KEAN'S PRODUCTION OF "SARDANAPALUS."
The hall of Nimrod, designed by F. Lloyds.
(Princess's Theatre, 1853.)

The scholar, so soon to lay his gown upon the shoulders of Charles Kean, had entered the theatre, and the way was open to the productions of Irving and of Tree.

Settings, too, changed with the costumes, and here we are able to distinguish clearly those three romantic tendencies noted above—love of the past, realism, and delight in the gloomy or grand. It may be well to take these in order. The love of the past is to be seen most clearly in the work of Capon, a scenic designer who sincerely tried to be exact. For Drury Lane about the year 1794 he painted various sets, mostly in Gothic style, endeavouring, in so far as lay in his power, to provide pictures of various buildings as these might have appeared to an inhabitant of the Middle Ages. Being an artist with a passion for "the ancient architecture of this country," he strove to achieve absolute exactitude. Indeed, he formed "a distinct feature" among scenic designers, "like the *black letter* class of a library." If Capon represents the romantic love of the past, his younger contemporary, Loutherbourg, an Alsatian artist patronized by Garrick, represents other qualities making up the romantic temper. In two things chiefly was Loutherbourg interested— the grand in Nature and the endeavour to express that grandeur in the most realistic terms possible. During one vacation he paid a visit—with a note-book—to Derbyshire, and returned to create what must then have been thrillingly realistic settings for a pantomime entitled *Harlequin of the Peak*;

similar scenes were provided for the spectacular
Christmas Tale, in which there appeared

> a sudden transition in a forest scene, where the
> foliage varies from green to blood colour. This
> contrivance was entirely new, and the effect
> was produced by placing different coloured
> silks in the flies or side scenes, which turned
> on a pivot, and with lights behind, which so
> illumined the stage, as to give the effect of
> enchantment.

Precisely such lighting effects, established during his period of work at Drury Lane, aided him
in his show of the Eidophusikon, referred to above.
Both Capon and Loutherbourg, with their lesser
associates, reflect the current interest in the
gloomy. The darkness of the mountains appeared in the work of the latter, while Capon's
Gothic buildings easily lend themselves to this
mood. Ruined castles, dimly lit cathedrals, dark
groves—these gradually took the place of the conventionally regular settings in Augustan taste.

Already it has been said that before 1800 these
efforts were only tentative ; but the gradual
popularization of the new methods rests to the
credit (or otherwise) of the eighteenth century.
The following age opened to see the older style
lingering on but now despised, and from Kemble,
through Macready and Charles Kean, on to Irving
and Tree, is one steady line of progression. More
and more the actor-managers turn to ancient records, old prints, the works of the early masters ;

Victoria and Albert Museum.

A DESIGN FOR CHARLES KEAN'S PRODUCTION OF "THE WINTER'S TALE."
A design by T. Grieves for the dance of shepherds and shepherdesses
in Act IV., Scene iii. (Princess's Theatre, 1856.)

more and more do they tend to regard historical
accuracy as of greater importance than æsthetic
beauty or symbolic appeal. A brief scrutiny of
Charles Kean's notes to his revived plays of
Shakespeare indicates clearly how far this movement had developed by the fifties of the century.
Kean's attitude was as much that of the school-
master and of the museum lecturer as that of the
actor-manager. In bidding farewell to his supporters after nine years of Shakespearian revivals,
he congratulated himself on having " so blended
. . . historical accuracy with pictorial effect that
instruction and amusement " at his theatre had
gone hand in hand ; he had made, he declared,
his theatre " a school as well as a recreation."
All this is strictly true. His introductions to the
printed texts are heavy with learning, and the
running commentaries bristle with the names of
obscure authorities. In the Victoria and Albert
Museum is preserved a collection of designs executed for his management, and from these may be
seen how faithfully and scrupulously he reproduced the very best and most authentic of original
models.

From this time on, care above all things was
expended upon these major dramatic productions.
Writing in 1891 of Browning's *Strafford* (1837)
Lady Martin (Helena Faucit) thought fit to observe
that

the play was mounted in all matters with
great care. Modern critics seem to have little

knowledge of the infinite pains bestowed in all respects before their day upon the representation of historical and Shakespearian plays.

This judgment is amply borne out by an examination of contemporary records. No doubt some theatres maintained primitive traditional devices, so that even in 1881 a commentator could refer to the " absurd or ludicrous " sight of " a table and two chairs moving on the scene, of themselves apparently, but drawn on by a cord," or " more singular still . . . on the prompter's whistle being heard, the table hurrying off at one side, the sofa and chairs at the other." Such primitive devices were rapidly becoming demoded, and by the time of Charles Kean had almost completely given way to fresh standards of workmanship.

Archæological research in the theatre no doubt reached its zenith in the time of Charles Kean, but it by no means died after his retirement. Kean had striven to instruct by making his painstaking mock antiques alluringly beautiful, and this pictorial appeal was made by many a later manager. Three decades after Kean had started his career at the Princess's Theatre, Henry Irving staged the first of those elaborate revivals for which he became so famous. In the *Romeo and Juliet* of 1882 he presented a series of spectacularly beautiful stage pictures. As the critic of *Dramatic Notes* wrote at the time, after describing the settings in the earlier acts :

One might have thought that scenic art could go no further, but the street in Mantua, in the fifth act, revealed a picture of great beauty ; and the tomb scene, with its entrance down several flights of steps, leading from the roof, was a marvel of scenic success, and the tableau at the conclusion of the play brought to a close one of the grandest spectacular representations of a Shakespearian play that has ever been presented.

In these productions Irving pursued Louther-bourg's path. He it was who first had the idea of changing his scenes in darkness, and to him more than any other we owe the darkened auditorium for the greater heightening of the stage effects. The style reached its zenith ten years later in *Henry VIII*. For this production the settings alone cost over £10,000. It may be said, indeed, that of the two aims of Charles Kean—splendour and accuracy—Irving, taking over both, tended to stress the former element ; his contemporary, Beerbohm Tree, was to provide a complement to his efforts, without in any way minimizing the magnificence of scenic display, by stressing the latter. Both followed in the line marked out by Kean in 1850, who, in turn, had taken the path half trodden out by a series of managers from the fatal time when Macklin first thought of his Scots kilt.

This archæological accuracy, of course, rarely intrudes into the sphere of comedy, but a cognate movement soon led the lighter drama in the same path. Realism was in the air; it might be the realism of historical pictures or the realism of ordinary life, but whatever form it took, it impressed itself on all minds. When tragedy was given correctness of atmosphere, comedy hastened to join its sister muse, casting off the old traditional comic garments and clothing itself in the fashions of the day.

For a time it seemed uncertain exactly what particular form that clothing would assume. At the Olympic under Madame Vestris various innovations had been introduced, and, inspired by the enthusiasm of J. R. Planché, burlesque and extravaganza took on fresh, delightful and, strangely enough, " correct " habiliments. Scenic splendour ruled here as at Kean's Princess's; laughter and tragic awe alike became tricked out in the visually magnificent. This movement, however, barely affected, or could affect, ordinary comedy, which, dragging itself with difficulty along, remained largely untouched by these newer movements. For comedy there was a potential demand, but no one so far had come to transform its artificial sentimentalities, inherited from the eighteenth century, into terms acceptable to Victorian England. Surveying the condition of the stage in 1865, John Hare found things in " a parlous state." Phelps was appearing at Drury Lane " in a destined to be short-lived production of Shakespeare's *King John* "; Mr. and Mrs. Charles Mathews were at the Haymarket; Charles Reade's *It's Never Too Late to Mend* was being

Victoria and Albert Museum.

A DESIGN BY HAWES CRAVEN FOR IRVING'S PRODUCTION OF
"HENRY VIII." (LYCEUM THEATRE, 1892.)

presented at the Princess's ; at the Adelphi Jefferson thrilled audiences in *Rip Van Winkle* ; and at the Lyceum Fechter was performing in *The Watch Cry*. As Hare noted, most of the plays that were not classics revived were poor, and the playgoers proved singularly apathetic. Yet that very apathy resulted from the seeds of discontent which had been variously sown from 1840 onwards. A lesson in romantic acting was being provided by Fechter for the old-fashioned school of playgoers ; and Sothern had been engaged in providing a similar lesson in the sphere of comedy. Lord Lytton and Dion Boucicault, moreover, had suggested new things in dramatic form. It only needed some one with keen sense of what the modern audiences demanded to bring these seeds to fruition.

The " some one " was Tom Robertson, whose *Society* saw its première in this very year, 1865. Produced by Bancroft and Marie Wilton (later Sir Squire and Lady Bancroft), *Society* immediately caught the attention of contemporaries, so that from it may truly be traced the rise of that comedy-drama so characteristic of the later nineteenth century. Its success, and the success of its followers, was, of course, due not merely to the skill of the dramatist ; largely contributing to its appeal was the strictly naturalistic method employed in the production—a method that bears the same relation to comedy as did Kemble's *King John* of 1823 to the tragic and historical drama. The setting aimed at reproducing reality faithfully : real door-knobs appeared on what had hitherto been merely painted flats ; and furniture appropriate to the settings called for by the play graced the boards. With the production of *Society* stage realism, in the narrower sense of that term, became established in the place of earlier conventionalism, and audiences which, in the first decades of the century, had thrilled to the romantic wonders of the new stage-spectacle, suddenly found a fresh joy in contemplating the merely drab.

The Robertsonian comedy, dependent upon real-life accuracy of settings, with ceilinged rooms, firm walls, and veritable door-knobs that actually turned, thus definitely paved the way for the Independent Theatre and its famous productions of Ibsen in the last decade of the century. The whole of the movement from Robertson to Pinero and Jones is characterized by this one common aim —the reproducing of the real on the stage. One must recognize that the novelty of the method itself contributed much to the awakening interest in the theatre which is so marked a feature of late Victorian society, that, too, important dramas rose directly out of the enthusiasm thus engendered ; on the other hand, the reflection cannot be avoided that the idea dominating the minds of managers and of public alike reached absurd proportions. Typical of the mood engendered in this time is the procedure of " Jemmy " White, one-time manager of the theatre at Nottingham. When he essayed the rôle of

Othello or that of Zanga in *The Revenge*, or even that of Mungo in *The Padlock*, he insisted on covering with black not only his face and arms but his whole body. " This," he is reported to have said, " gave him a better idea what a black man should feel and be." Jemmy White was by no means an odd eccentric ; he was merely giving expression in one particular way to that general desire for realism which in this age made men forget those words of Schiller which should be engraved over the doorway of every playhouse :

> Lightly built is the car of Thespis ; like Charon's barque, it carries only shades and phantoms ; and if rude life presses abroad, the frail craft, suited only for the tread of flitting ghosts, threatens to capsize ; if Nature triumphs, Art is overcome.

These words have an eternal truth, yet, even while noting the ridiculous lengths to which scenic designers and actor-managers went in their quest, even while condemning this realism—as it must be condemned—we have to remember that, in its time, it served its purpose in the development of theatrical art. By 1750 the conventionalism of the Augustan age was no longer a vital conventionalism ; its spirit had fled, and only the dry bones remained. It was necessary that some new life force should seize hold of the theatre, and that new life force was found in the realistic movement. We do not want any more realism to-day, for its spirit, too, has fled, but for the nineteenth century nothing could have been better than this artistic dose. Realistic dramas were wanted by the age, and those realistic dramas could come only when a suitable theatrical framework was provided for their interpretation. The reform in comic garments gave Tom Robertson the means of achieving his effects; the innovations of Robertson, improved upon by others, established the basis for the plays of John Galsworthy.

Considerable space has been given here to a discussion of this subject because the settings of the nineteenth century are the most noticeable and influential things theatrically in that period. Such a statement, however, does not imply that these furnished everything which we can find of interest in the course of these hundred years. In a variety of different ways the nineteenth-century stage was breaking with the past and so helping to create the stage of to-day. Here, one thing above all stands out important, and that is the so-called " Freedom of the Theatres." The nineteenth century opened with a heritage from the past. Theoretically, only two playhouses (Drury Lane and Covent Garden) were entitled regularly to present the spoken drama, although by 1800 there was associated with them the Theatre Royal in the Haymarket, which, granted a " summer " licence, was permitted to give dramatic fare of any kind during the vacation. In practice, however, these theatres by no means provided all the entertainment for contemporary

Londoners. Already attention has been drawn to the presence in the eighteenth century of a number of " minor " theatres, the repertoire of which had consisted largely of pantomime and spectacle. It is in the years immediately following that those minors sprang into real prominence, their growth of power being dependent upon three things—mismanagement of the larger theatres, the growth of the playgoing public, and the development of that peculiar and almost undefinable dramatic type called the burletta.

The major playhouses, as we have seen, had already turned to spectacle as a source of income ; spectacle being expensive, both Drury Lane and Covent Garden were enlarged until it was impossible for the audience to hear any words save those that were shouted, and difficult even to see anything except massed effects on the stage. For appearances' sake, certainly, they continued to produce the regular spoken drama, but on this a blight seemed to have fallen. Monotonous comedy of a sentimental kind and tragedy full of turgid rhetoric could make but little appeal to spectators on whom had fallen at least the fringe of romantic enthusiasm ; while the fact that these plays could hardly find efficient interpretation in the vast new theatres rendered them doubly dull. In spite of the presence of many outstanding actors —Kemble, Kean, Macready among them—Drury Lane and Covent Garden declined, and spectators tended more and more to seek their diversion elsewhere.

That " elsewhere " was, of course, the minor
theatre, which, in addition to other advantages,
had for the poorer-class audiences which had
taken the place of the upper-middle-class playgoers
the merit of having a kind of homely atmosphere.
With the support of the public the lesser managers
made every effort to develop and expand. Realiz-
ing that they were permitted to present musical
pieces, they started experimenting with the " burletta." Originally, the burletta was, as the name
implies, a short burlesque opera, generally concerned with the comic presentation of Greek gods
and heroes ; but soon it increased its scope and
became simply an eccentric musical farce. Gradually the musical element was permitted to decline,
although to the end it was retained in the form of
at least a tinkling piano. Burlettas, having vigour
and good laughable business, prospered, and the
major theatres adopted them, as they had previously
adopted pantomimic spectacle. Then Drury
Lane made a fatal blunder : in its regular repertoire was *Tom Thumb*, Fielding's burlesque to
which Kane O'Hara had added a number of
lyrical ditties ; carelessly, and in spite of the fact
that it contained spoken dialogue, it was billed as a
" burletta." Immediately the minors seized their
opportunity. If *Tom Thumb*, consisting of spoken
dialogue and song, was a burletta, then they could
dare to present a certain amount of spoken dialogue
in their shows. It is impossible here to outline the
growth of the burletta from this date; sufficient is
it to notice that within a few years we find the

official Licenser of Plays, George Colman the
Younger, declaring that a burletta must be defined
as a play of three acts, including not less than five
songs ; not a word was now said concerning the
subject-matter or treatment.   The implications
are obvious.   *Macbeth* arranged in three acts and
with some musical addition became a burletta ;
so did *The School for Scandal* similarly treated.
In other words, the minor theatres were now free
to play practically anything they chose.   Generally,
however, they chose, not the dull " legitimate "
drama to which the major theatres clung majestically, but more thrilling pieces of the melodramatic kind, or lighter entertainment in the form
of joyous farce and burlesque extravaganza.
Their power rapidly increased, and, as it ex-
panded, that of Drury Lane and Covent Garden
declined.   The scope of their efforts, and the part
they played in the London theatrical world during
the first four decades of the century, may be
gauged by their very number.   Besides Sadler's
Wells, The Sans-Souci, and the Royal Circus,
inherited from before 1800, nearly twenty such
houses appeared between 1800 and 1840.   *Astley's*
was built in 1804, *The Adelphi* (first known as
The Sans-Pareil) in 1806, *The Olympic* in the same
year, *The Lyceum* in 1809 (called also *The English
Opera House*), *The Queen's* (variously styled *The
Regency* and *The Prince of Wales's*) also in 1809.
The following two decades witnessed the arising
of many rivals : *The Surrey* in 1811, *The Royal
Coburg* (now *The Old Vic*) in 1818, *The Pavilion* in

1829, *The Garrick*, *The Princess's*, and *The Strand* in 1830. The thirties, too, energetically carried on the tradition with *The City* in 1831, *The Orange Street Theatre* (Chelsea) about the same time, *The Albion* (alias *The New Queen's*), *King's Cross* (also known as *The Regent*), *The New Royal Sussex* (which went by a variety of names : *The Pavilion*, *The Portman*, *The Royal Marylebone*), and *The Westminster*, all in 1832, *The Globe* in 1833, *The Royal Borough* and *The Royal Kent* in 1834, *The Royal Standard*, *St. James's* and *The City of London* in 1835. Meanwhile the great Drury Lane of 1812 was hovering near bankruptcy, and Covent Garden was thinking of abandoning plays for opera.

Eventually, by about the year 1840, it became apparent to every thoughtful man that the situation was a ridiculous one, and in 1843 came the final release of the minor theatres from their restrictions. Provided their plays were duly licensed by the Lord Chamberlain, they could present precisely the same fare as had been permitted to the major houses. Perhaps immediately this did not mean much, but ultimately the effects of the Act of 1843 were of enormous significance. Phelps could conduct a famous series of Shakespearian performances at Sadler's Wells, and later Sir Henry Irving could make famous one of the old minor theatres, the Lyceum. The way was opened for the development of more serious drama at any one of a score of London theatres. Short-sighted managers of Drury Lane could no longer maintain a foolish monopoly.

No more complete break with the past could be imagined, and, whatever we have to say against the nineteenth-century theatre, we must at least give it the credit for seeking after and securing a certain freedom and liberty.

Strangely enough, however, the passing of the Act of 1843 seemed for the moment to halt the rapid theatre-building which had distinguished the preceding forty years. After the opening of *The New Royalty* (1840), *The Britannia* (1841), and *The East London* (1844), there was a complete lull until the appearance of *The Royalty* in 1861. By the sixties, however, a new audience again was arising, and with the success of Robertson's *Society* demand was being made for playhouses of an intimate kind wherein the new realistic drama might be presented. Without mentioning the many suburban houses, we realize that the years between 1865 and 1900 were even more active in this regard than the earlier decades. *The Gaiety* and *The Globe* came in 1868, and *The Charing Cross* (later called *The Folly*) in 1869 ; *The Opera Comique* and *The Vaudeville* followed in 1870 ; then came *The Court* (known as *The New Chelsea Theatre*) in 1871, *The Criterion* in 1874, *The Imperial* in 1876. The years 1881 and 1882 saw the opening of *The Comedy*, *The Savoy*, *The Avenue*, and *The Novelty*. *The Prince of Wales's* was built in 1884, and during the seasons 1888-1889 *Terry's*, *The Lyric*, *The Shaftesbury*, and *The Garrick*. The nineties continued the good work with *The Royal English Opera House* (known also as *The Palace*, 1891), *The Duke of York's* (or *The Trafalgar Square*, 1892), *Daly's* (1893), *Her Majesty's* (1897), and *Wyndham's* (1899). Nor should it be forgotten that many of the unreferred-to suburban theatres, such as *The Elephant and Castle* (1872) and *The Lyric, Hammersmith* (1891), played a not unimportant part in London's theatrical affairs. After years of perplexing monopoly the playhouse had won its freedom.

Freedom and liberty, too, were not confined to the theatres and their repertories. The actors shared in the general emancipation. During the entire course of the eighteenth century and for the first decades of the nineteenth, the players had occupied an anomalous position. Fêted and welcomed in certain aristocratic houses, they yet remained beings apart. To say that a man was an actor was to place him in a very definite social category, and although a Garrick, a Mrs. Siddons, and an Edmund Kean might mix with society of the highest, yet that category was not one of very imposing pretensions. Often the actors themselves emphasized the distinction between them and others, both by adopting a kind of Crummlesesque histrionic demeanour and by dressing themselves peculiarly. The distinction was the more noticeable in view of ecclesiastical opinion. In spite of the fact that a few clergymen contributed plays to the stage between 1700 and 1840, the Church as a whole, animated by ancient prejudices, held aloof from contact with the theatre. Periodically, embittered ministers of the gospel published fierce diatribes against the playhouses and those associated with their evil ways, and by their influence kept a great section of the moral middle-class from having anything to do with that which Prynne in 1632 had designated the haunt of the devil.

After 1840 this attitude began to change, and, so far as England was concerned, the motive power behind the alteration of opinion is to be traced to Queen Victoria. After many years of German-speaking and illiterate monarchs, Victoria brought something fresh to the throne; and by summoning Charles Kean to perform at Court she revived a tradition of the seventeenth century. Seeing the Queen thus patronize the players, society soon followed suit, and even the Church hastened to revise its opinions. The natural consequence was that the performers themselves reacted to the changed conditions. Instead of trying to remain distinct and separate, the player now endeavoured to be a gentleman. His clothes were as impeccably, as modishly and as modestly cut as my lord's, and his conversation became a good deal more polite than Tennyson's. As a guest, not as a notorious curiosity, he was welcomed at dinner-table and in boudoir; indeed, he himself soon was able, with Henry Irving, to boast his own independent title. Irving's knighthood is to be regarded as a symbol of what had happened to the actor during these years.

Quite naturally, too, these altered social con-

ditions had an effect upon histrionic style. Up
to 1840 methods of performance had been flam-
boyant and exaggerated. Edmund Kean, both in
his social life and in his artistic, proves typical of
these years. Although acclaimed as more realistic
than Kemble, his acting style, to judge from all
the accounts that have come down to us, must
have been artificial in the extreme. The only
difference between the two seems to have been
that whereas the former was intellectually rhetorical, the latter was passionately so. Kean, according to Macready, "hurried you along in his reso-
lute course with a spirit that brooked no delay";
he literally carried people off their feet, and by a
combination of seeming naturalism and almost
lyrical frenzy captured the romantically inclined
sentiment of his age. In social life Kean wanted
always to be the lionized hero. Overweening and
contemptuous in his success, he definitely placed
a barrier between himself and others.

Comic methods during these early years were
of a like sort. Munden and Liston must have been
notable performers, but their grimacing and
exaggeration of dress and of gesture placed them
clearly in the sphere of farce. The former unquestionably "lost half his proper effect, by the
very strength of his powers"; writing in 1865
Dr. Doran thought that "the breadth of his
acting is now hardly conceivable." Likening him
to Hogarth, Lamb describes his method as "the
grand grotesque of farce" and emphasizes the
extraordinary play of his features :

There is one face of Farley, one face of
Knight, one (but what a one it is !) of Liston ;
but Munden has none that you can properly
pin down, and call *his*. When you think he has
exhausted his battery of looks, in unaccountable
warfare with your gravity, suddenly he sprouts
out an entirely new set of features, like Hydra.
He is not one, but legion ; not so much a
comedian, as a company. If his name could be
multiplied like his countenance, it might fill a
play-bill. He, and he alone, literally *makes
faces*.

Liston's whole tendency lay, too, in a similar
direction ; in regular comic parts he may have
acted, but he made them into farcical caricatures.
Where Munden hilariously called for laughter by
the boldness of his gestures and of his mouthings,
Liston sought for the same means by a studied
seriousness and melancholy of demeanour, ex-
aggerating his solemnity as the other exaggerated
his hilarious fun. Typical, too, of this time was
Robert William Elliston, the exponent of the
gentleman in comedy ; magnificent, no doubt,
and worthy Charles Lamb's ecstatic praise, but
like his companions refusing to bow to the
natural. His dress, consisting of blue coat, white
waistcoat, and white knee-breeches (whatever the
character happened to be), served as an index for
his approach. His " gentlemen " were set on a
plane far apart from that of any gentleman in the
audience. Truly, it was his nature to be artificial,

and he strutted through his parts in a lordly
manner, achieving his results by a glorious farcical
vitality. The stage that Lamb knew and loved was
a tempestuous one, ruled by virtuosity and frankly
making play with the most ridiculous and absurd
effects.

Gradually comes a change. Edmund Kean
cedes his place to Macready, who, although still
essentially unrealistic in his approach, tones down
the almost frantic mannerisms of his predecessor.
Comparing the two, Hazlitt praised in Kean
" the individual bursts of feeling " and " the deep
and accumulating tide of passion," but criticized
his lack of authority and " stateliness "; Macready,
he thought, failed in the enunciation of passion,
being too " calm and collected "—a finer declaimer
than Kean, but less emotionally effective as an
actor. Calmness and good taste were succeeding
to the realms of impassioned frenzy; a con-
servative Tennyson now wore the mantle of a
revolutionary Shelley. " If Mr. Kean is the most
intensely human, and Mr. Kemble the most
classical," thought a contemporary critic, " Mr.
Macready is the most romantic of actors," and
the word romantic here signified something less
exciting and less enthusiastic than the romantic
tendencies of earlier years. Macready won his
results, R. H. Horne tells us, by " long study " :

His conception is slow, and by degrees; nor
does it ever attain beyond a certain point.
That point is the extremity of all that his study

and practice can discover and embody. . . .
He has no revelations of genius, no inspirations
except those which are unconsciously " given
off " at times from great physical energies. If
he had any such revelations, he would adopt
them doubtfully, and partially, and so defeat
their essential meaning. But when he does embrace the whole of a character (such as William
Tell, Coriolanus, Iago, Cardinal Wolsey, King
John), he leaves little undone, and all the rest
to admire, in the highest degree. He dresses
to perfection. He is the only man on the stage
who seems to have a fine eye for true harmony
of colour. Sometimes he has allowed splendid
dresses to be destroyed by an equally splendid
background of similar colour, but never when he
himself is in front of it. . . . There is great finish
in all he does—a definite aim, clearly worked
out—and those who find little to admire in his
acting, the fault is in them.

Following Kemble, Macready spent much time
in preparation for " the ' getting up ' of dramas,"
and in this, as well as in his tasteful, refined histrionic style, he proved the master of Charles Kean,
exploiter of "gentlemanly melodrama." That very
phrase is an index to the later Kean's proclivities.
Where Edmund Kean had never even approached
the fringe of the gentlemanly in his art or of his life,
on this his son consistently concentrated. Macready had become intimately familiar with London's poets and men of letters ; Charles Kean

attended Court and mixed with highest society. Suddenly the stage became polite.

Not, of course, that the old style quite died out. Irving belonged to the earlier romantic tradition. Never quite did he lose a certain grandness of manner and eccentricity of approach. Irving was a great and influential force in the late nineteenth century, and his artistic descendants are still to be found on the playhouse boards; but in reality cricket-playing F. R. Benson, inclined to present Shakespeare's heroes as if they had just obtained their Blues, is far more representative of the new school that had come into being. Benson could not quite make Shakespeare a gentleman, but he did his best.

With the picture-frame theatre had come an approximation of dramatic fiction and of life.

In comedy, too, the methods established by the Bancrofts at the Prince of Wales's won a victory over the earlier styles. J. B. Buckstone had carried on the low comedy tradition set by Lamb's favourites, but soon other traditions were to be laid down. Little Frederick Robson, with his Chaplinesque admixture of farcical buffoonery and pathetic seriousness, brought an element of feeling into his burlesques which clearly served to bridge the chasm between the old and the new, and in this he was followed directly by J. L. Toole. The real change, however, came with the Robertsonian comedies. The comic clown abandoned his grotesque garments and modified his actions; laughter he sought to raise by a turn of the wrist, preferring that to the farcical merriment created by a somersault. Acutely, Sir Arthur Pinero in *Trelawny of the Wells* has shown how entry into the palaces of Mayfair and Belgravia caused the actors to find their former parts ridiculous and meaningless; how a Rose Trelawny could no longer take joy in the bold, artificial ways of the ancient stage, but discovered a rich world in parts which, because drawn from life, reminded spectators of members of their own families. The Bancrofts themselves and those, such as John Hare, associated with them strove to eliminate the grotesque and stress the natural. If a Sir Charles Hawtrey pursued the course of Robson and Toole, the theatrical highway was now in the hands of men and women who sometimes were inclined to pursue naturalism so far as to become inaudible. New standards had been established, and the stage was possessed by the refined urbanity of a Sir George Alexander.

CHAPTER VII

THE MODERN PERIOD

WRITING in the nineties of last century, Henry Arthur Jones hailed the " Renaissance of the English Theatre," a renaissance which, like that earlier renaissance of the sixteenth century, was not confined to one land. If the English playhouse produced a Jones, a Pinero, a Wilde, and a Shaw, abroad there flourished Ibsen and Strindberg, Tchechov and Andreiev, Hauptmann and Sudermann, Brieux and Maeterlinck. Limiting our gaze to no one country, we may confidently assert that, since 1600, no period has shown a richer display of dramatic talent than the years 1890 to 1910.

Partly this sudden access of strength has been due to the increased interest in the theatre among all classes in the community. In England there was the aristocratic Restoration playhouse, the genteel upper-middle-class playhouse of the eighteenth century, and the largely lower-class playhouse of the early nineteenth century ; during all that time from 1660 to 1860 nothing had approached the universal and representative audience before which Shakespeare brought his *Hamlet* and his *Midsummer Night's Dream.* The conditions between 1880 and 1900 became ripe for just such an awakening as actually the theatre experienced during the nineties.

Partly, too, this awakening resulted from the achievement of a new artistic ideal. There is always mental and emotional excitement accompanying the progress of some fresh aim in art, and for these years realism furnished a style of this kind towards which nearly all men strove. For centuries the theatre had remained purely conventional; now audiences saw, with wonder, that the playhouse need not lead them into strange realms and make them listen to unfamiliar accents, but could present well-known firesides to the eye, and to the ear thoroughly commonplace conversation. Such a realistic method could be finally consummated only in a theatre kin to that possessed by the eighties, for dramatic realism demands theatrical machinery of a highly complex sort. So long as a change of set required no more than the running in of a set of wings and the lowering of a back-cloth, no elaborate system of control was called for; but in these days of built-up sets, sets which abandoned the two-dimensional in favour of the three-dimensional, the older methods of scene-shifting became, if not completely futile, at least cumbersome and inefficient. By 1880 the theatre was fairly well equipped for the realist director, and by 1900 there was little left for him to ask. Theatre architects now normally made provision for lofty grids so that scenes might be raised to the flies, and, not content with that, devoted their energies to inventing means for making stages turn, sink, and slide, rise up in sections or descend in mass. No longer was the stage a set of " boards " placed on supporting bars, with a trap or two for supernatural effects ; it was composed of many portions, taking shape now as a series of vast steps, now as a flat forward area and a great pit behind. On such a stage scenes might be changed rapidly, for in a playhouse built in this wise any particular setting could be erected underneath the stage proper or at its side ; the act finished, part of the stage floor might sink, bearing its scenery with it, and, sliding to the side, leave room for the raising of the new scene to its place. At his command the director might have a monstrous machine responsive to every touch of a control.

Nor was this all. Never had the theatre possessed such an array of mechanical and scientific devices, associated with each possible branch of play production. Gas was an improvement on oil, but electricity brought with it untold advantages. By its means the powers of the machinist were increased a thousandfold. His control became more exact ; the effects he secured were almost instantaneous ; he could completely extinguish one set of globes and bring them on again without the laborious toil of relighting. Above all, he could place his source of illumination where he willed, troubling his head neither with thoughts of unwieldy lead tubing nor with fears of conflagration. With electricity, too, came many subsidiary inventions. The old " magic lantern " found a home for itself in the playhouse, furnishing, in the use of the Schwabe-Hasait system, a set of cloud-effects hardly to be imagined in days when clouds were merely painted on flat canvas borders. Chemical research has likewise been introduced to the stage, and, if we will, we may now gaily turn our actors into negroes or whites as we move our switches this way or that. In this modern theatre the last word has been said concerning that realism which began to grow with the rise of romantic aspirations in the second half of the eighteenth century. The roaring of the lions in the Zoo may be carried in a gramophone record to the playhouse ; the infinity of sky is presented in the cyclorama. We might well be under the blue expanse itself or standing before the bars of the cage, instead of sitting comfortably in our plush-covered stalls.

Achievement secured, where do we now stand ? There are many contemporaries who gaze with dismal eyes on the stage and prognosticate its ruin, and in general these point with gravely accusing fingers at the cinema. For between the time when the renaissance of the theatre in Europe created a fresh enthusiasm and our present days the cinema was invented, introduced to the public and rendered triumphant. Over the entire world the film has swept and inevitably has carried with it thousands of the theatre's former supporters. In London alone there are sufficient " picture houses " to seat a quarter of the teeming millions in the metropolis. Complaints are rife that the

presentation of plays has become a hazardous
business, and that gradually the stage will be compelled to cede its place to the screen. So much
easier is it for members of the public to go to the
films than to go to plays, the entrance charges are
so much less, the films have to offer so many more
attractions to theatre artists—these and other
causes of the cinema's success are obvious; there
is no need to search obscurely for reasons of the
cinema's popularity or for instances of the way in
which it has suborned talent from the stage.
This success, deem many, is not yet at its height;
the last of the theatres, they opine, will soon be
with us and gazed on as a curio until it, too, gives
way and is fitted up like the rest with the latest
sound-recording apparatus.

These conditions, of course, are not peculiar
to England; and, since they affect the whole of
Europe and America, a word may perhaps be
said in general discussion before we come to
consider the more precise conditions applying to
the stage in London and the English provinces.
One thing at once makes us pause. Theatre
building has not ceased since the cinema's introduction. Certainly many of the older theatres
have gone out of commission, and certainly, too,
several of the newly erected houses have, within
a few months or years, been turned into " picture
palaces "; but even so the record of theatrical
architecture coupled with that which demonstrates
the number of playhouses currently open in
London, New York, and Paris indicates that the

play is, somehow, still holding its own. Between
1900 and 1913 about a dozen new theatres were
built in London—*The Apollo* (1901), *The New*
(1903), *The Scala* (1905), *The Strand* (known as
The Waldorf, 1905), *The Royalty* (1905), *The
Globe* (known as *Hicks's*, 1906), *The Queen's* (1907),
The Playhouse (1907), *The Kingsway* (1907), *The
Little* (1910), *The Prince's* (1911), *The Ambassador's*
(1913). True, some of these merely took the place
of other earlier buildings, but against that fact
we have another, that the list, to be complete,
ought to include several suburban houses, such as
The King's, Hammersmith (1902) and *The Wimble-
don* (1910). Since 1913, activity in this direction
has not entirely waned. *St. Martin's* opened in
1916, *The London Pavilion* in 1918, *The Winter
Garden* in 1919 ; *The Everyman* (1920), *The New
Oxford* (1921), *The Fortune* (1924), *The Q* (1924),
The Carlton (1927), *The Embassy* (1928), and *The
Piccadilly* (1928) followed. Even the last few years
have not been idle, and we number among Lon-
don's houses of entertainment *The Duchess* (1929),
The Dominion (1929), *The Phœnix* (1930), *The
Cambridge* (1930), *Prince Edward's* (1930), *The
Whitehall* (1930), *The Saville* (1931), and the new
Sadler's Wells (1931).

That the cinema has drawn away many persons
from the theatre cannot be denied, and that this
attendance at the " picture houses " was due not
merely to the novelty of the newly invented form
seems proved by the continued appeal made by
the films. The films have come to stay ; that we

must accept.   On the other hand, two considera-
tions there are which must be taken into account.
The first is that, as the cinema has developed
within the last few years, a greater sense of the
particular qualities belonging to the two forms of
entertainment becomes apparent.   The cinema
may have produced much of little value and at the
same time may have aped the manners and methods
of the stage ; but there is every reason to believe
that, within the next decade or so, we shall witness
a clarification of cinematic ideals and so come to
recognize the film, not as an opponent of or as a
mere borrower from the play, but as a cognate art-
form, with its own independent aims and purposes.
This, in turn, will demand a reconsideration of the
theatre's ideals, and a consequent determination
to exploit what legitimately the theatre may
accomplish and the cinema fail to secure.

The second consideration is the fact that the
cinema's public is composed not only of those
who were former supporters of the stage.   The
film, by its cheapness and its general appeal, has
brought within the walls of the " picture house "
thousands who, had they lived twenty years ago,
would never have thought of seeking entertainment outside of their homes, their public-houses
and their cafés.   This has meant that a far larger
section of the community has acquired a taste for
entertainment of the sort which is provided by
cinema and by theatre alike ; and signs are not
lacking that, once drawn within the orbit of the
film, many of these new spectators are beginning

to explore the theatre's realms. Such a playhouse as The Old Vic owes its popularity partly at least to the support of an otherwise film-going public.

One may suggest, therefore, that pessimistic forebodings of disaster are hardly justified in any general terms ; the theatre, by its closeness of appeal and by its intimacy of artistic presentation, is never likely to be vanquished by the cinema's two-dimensional method of expression. Yet, to preserve its popularity, the theatre requires to consider carefully the rôle it is to essay in succeeding years. To succeed, it needs to do more than drift, as at present it is drifting ; the time is calling for a fresh enthusiasm and a keener sense of purpose. No doubt much is demanded in the realm of purely material reorganization ; the luxury of the cinema must be met by a new ease in the theatre. Many reforms are demanded, even in apparently trivial things. Sixpence is not a large sum of money, but to many it is irritating, after paying fairly highly for seats not too comfortable, to be forced into the purchase of a programme, which often conceals its valid information amid a mass of alcoholic advertisements. A ridiculous extreme was reached in the recent *Close Quarters*, for which the programme contained (on two widely spaced pages) mention of but a couple of performers, of the producer, of three scenes (Act III. being " the same as Act II."), of the scene designer and of the maker of the heroine's costumes. There were twenty-five pages of advertisements. A trivial

thing, perhaps, but if a host is arranging a party
and spends fifty shillings or more for four seats,
that triviality is apt at times to weigh heavily.
A camel's back can bear only so many stalks of
straw, and the little extras may well operate in
making a modern host consider whether, after all,
a proposal to go to the latest film (at a cost of about
a pound) might not prove as acceptable to his
guests as a visit to the theatre.

This material reorganization, however, is of
secondary importance, compared with the necessity of securing a fresh spiritual and artistic reorganization.   Gladly would we pay our extra
sixpences if the theatre were to provide that vital
enthusiasm already alluded to and that keen sense
of purpose.

First of all, a new style is demanded, and that
new style so far has not been given us.   While the
realistic movement was in process of growth, it
proved both stimulating and creative.   Now, however, that it has reached the fulfilment of its aims
and has achieved absolute mastery, this creativeness
and stimulus have vanished.   No longer do we
thrill to see some almost perfect simulation of the
natural, for, knowing what the theatre already has
accomplished, this is precisely what we have come
to expect.   Unemotionally we are prepared to
receive all that the scene-designer and the carpenter have in this way to offer ; no conscious
appreciation or mental effort accompanies our
acceptance of what they give to us.   Moreover,
the cinematic art so freely presented to us has

largely exploited a similar realism, and, having vast means at its command and a more easily controlled instrument, it can readily go beyond most of what the stage sets out to accomplish. Indifference, therefore, greets these attempts ; and theatrically indifference is ever fatal. The theatre, to live truly and well, must always provide the sudden excitement of unexpectedness, the thrill of the hitherto unknown and unlooked for. The truth is that in our modern stage we have reached the end of an evolutionary cycle. From the open-air playhouse of the Greeks, through the Elizabethan theatres on to those of the Restoration and the eighteenth century, the idea governing the development in structure has been that of obtaining greater and greater illusion. With the establishment of the picture-frame stage and with the aid of scientific invention we have come to an end. No more may we do in this direction ; there is nothing to strive for and no more to dream. An ideal has gone, and in its place nothing save what has now become a dull reality.

That this fact has been appreciated is proved by several attempts made during the last quarter century to find a completely new basis for theatrical production. On the Continent the vogue of the theatre of vast possibilities and almost limitless power of illusion has begun to pall, and various groping searches have been made in the direction of something lying utterly beyond its sphere. The machine theatre has aroused dissatisfaction, partly because it has grown to such dimensions as to place the director at the mercy of the machine, but chiefly because of the very fact that it can create too great an illusion. In all directions men have turned to seek for ways of escape. Some aim at absolute simplicity, and the small intimate theatre with a fixed decorative background becomes the heart's desire. Here the bare walls surrounding the stage are left revealed, and the action takes place on boards unadorned by any scenery. Here fantasy is given free play, and grotesque symbolic forms drive realism far off. Here are built up on the stage vast forms reproducing the idea, but not the actual shapes, of modern industrial machinery. The intimate theatre, the bare theatre, the impressionistic theatre, the constructivist theatre— all have been tried, and are still being tried, on the Continent at centres as widely apart as Rome and Moscow, Berlin and Paris.

All these various movements of reaction (or of revolution) are due to a widespread discontent both with the realistic and with the archæologically spectacular methods of the immediate past. In so far as they embody a desire for something new, they are to be welcomed ; but it must be confessed that up to the present no dominant style has arisen out of the experiments likely to take the place of the nineteenth-century styles. What we want is a theatre theatrical and not a theatre naturalistic ; but the several expressionistic and constructivist efforts have been accorded but a moderate welcome by the public at large. The experimentation is good, but, if the theatre is to gain success, it must proceed until a form is discovered apt, by its strength and the vitality of its appeal, to capture whole-heartedly the public's attention.

Although the Continental reactions are to be explained largely as the result of natural development of a general mood, yet two men there were who, as individuals, were largely responsible for their growth. One was Adolphe Appia, and the other, strangely enough, was an Englishman, Edward Gordon Craig. Both Appia and Craig revolted against the older theatre, and both endeavoured to provide settings for plays which should be simple, beautiful in proportion, significant in form, and innocent of that so-called " realistic " scene-painting which converts long strips of obvious canvas into very flat tree branches which wave uneasily with every wind that blows from the auditorium or succeeds in creating such an illusion that art is forgotten. The ideas put forward by these two men have been adopted, transformed, altered in almost every Continental country. The seeds they have sown have blossomed into a thousand flowers of diverse hues and varying shapes, for an idea in art does not necessarily produce but one expression. The idea is the stimulus to the imagination, and the idea of Gordon Craig lies as potent behind the most bizarre of Russian experiments as it does behind his own exquisite scene pictures.

That one of the two men who have been most instrumental in developing a new scenic art in Europe should have been born an Englishman

calls for comment, because the English theatre at
the present time is displaying a strange lack of
inventiveness and initiativeness. A very few
individual artists have far-sighted ideals ; a few
amateur or semi-amateur groups grope blindly
towards the light ; but a darkness of now out-
worn tradition hangs over the greater part of the
professional theatre. We consider ourselves very
daring if we deviate ever so slightly from established precedent, and progressive if we abandon
for a moment the naturalistic method. Otherwise,
we are content to drift aimlessly on. Old spectacularism is re-dished for modern tastes, and
" realistically " painted flats with appropriate
backgrounds form the regular stock-in-trade of
the playhouse. Occasional beauty, perhaps, is
secured, but occasional beauty is not enough in
art. Ugliness achieved in the making of an experiment ; æsthetic failure resultant upon the
following of a new ideal—these are far to be placed
above success in an antiquated style. No art may
flourish so long as it remains stagnant. Experimentation spells movement at least, and the English
theatre, lacking the spirit for experimentation, is
artistically and mentally moribund. Momentary
flashes of life simply serve to emphasize the
debility of the rest.

It cannot be too often asserted that the fortunes
of the theatre in every age depend ultimately upon
the spectators who attend that theatre. A small
minority in the audience cannot accomplish anything, nor can a band of artists unaided by the

public ; for the theatre is the most popular of all the arts, and takes its colour and tone immediately from those who enter to witness the performances. It is, therefore, the average English audience which is responsible for whatever forms their theatre assumes to-day. That average English audience is, unfortunately, uninformed, uncritical of all but the play and (less frequently) the actor, uninterested in the theatre either as an art or as a social force. The consequence is that, while the English theatre has been able to produce worthy dramatists, and while there has been there a fine and distinguished tradition in histrionic art, only rarely has England had a playhouse progressive in all those forms of artistic endeavour which together create the great and all-embracing art of the theatre. On the Continent, the theatre at its best is an absolute necessity of life. Men are willing to support it by taxation, both local and central. They demand their State theatres and generally they demand their municipal theatres. This is true, not only of great centres such as we find in Germany and France, but of the lesser states of Eastern Europe as well. In England any Government which proposed to establish a national playhouse would meet with a storm of indignant protest. No Ministry would risk its life in the attempt. There are enthusiasts here for a national theatre, but they do not represent the mass of the community. Their ideal is beyond the ideal of the crowd.

Another thing may be said of this theatre

audience. The English have always been suspicious of those forms of art which do not make an immediate and direct appeal to the intellect. They are essentially practical, and consequently they relish only the manifestations of art which they can understand easily and rationally. They can appraise the spoken words of a dramatist and they can argue logically about the interpretation of an actor. They can produce and understand great prose, and they can apply their intellects to the appreciation of poetry. This is probably the true explanation of a phenomenon which is at once apparent when we compare the art of England with the arts of other races and times. Greece found self-expression both in literature and sculpture ; France has found it in literature and painting ; Germany in literature and music ; Italy in literature, painting, and music. England takes artistic rank with these other countries in respect of its literature alone. A moral bias no doubt lurks behind this peculiarity. Art in its purest forms has absolutely nothing to do with decalogical morality ; but an Englishman thinks it has. He can at once appraise a work of literature from his own particular moral standpoint; but painting, particularly when it deals with pure form and colour, renders him uncomfortable and seems of no practical worth. As a result he likes to see in the theatre nothing but the old traditional realistic or semi-realistic forms to which he has grown thoroughly accustomed, and which can have no possible subversive influence.

Partly connected with this national tendency there is still another thing which is restraining development in the English theatrical world. Since the written text of a play is that part of a performance which makes most appeal to the intellect, audiences and theatre-workers alike tend to over-emphasize the rôle that is played by the dramatist, and to regard his works apart from the stage for which they were intended. It is forgotten that a drama achieves its fulfilment only when acted. The spoken word is an essential element in a great and vital theatre; but " the spoken word " has become for our present-day playhouse a fatal phrase. By emphasis upon that the dramatist becomes lord of all and occupies a position which overshadows the other artists concerned with theatrical performances. No doubt the dramatist is of principal importance; no doubt all respect should be given to his words; but the theatre does not exist for the sake of the dramatist; the dramatist exists only by virtue of and by the will of the theatre. A printed text of *Hamlet* is only partly alive. It does not assume its full existence until a body of actors in a theatre interpret the words written down on the printed page to an assembled audience. The play exists only in the theatre; but the converse is not true. The theatre may, if it will, do without the dramatist. A *commedia dell'arte* performance, perhaps in its own way the very essence of theatrical art, was innocent of the playwright. The dramatist lives not alone, as a poet does, and Shakespeare, one imagines, would have been of the first to endorse this statement. A theatrical performance is a form of art in which men and women, in one harmony, endeavour to express character and action upon the stage, and that performance makes its appeal as much to the eye as to the ear.

While the literary dramatist is regarded with esteem, paradoxically the theatre in England is treated, for the most part, as a mere amusement. One may readily agree that delight of this sort is intimately bound up with appreciation of the art of the stage. There is worth in farce and musical comedy, worth too in the thrill that comes from mystery dramas. These are all part of the theatre. But they should not be all. The theatre, most social of all the arts, should have an emotional, an intellectual, and an imaginative appeal beyond mere pleasure. Charles Kean was wrong in speaking of instruction in the playhouse, but there is a dilating of the spirit through art which has naught to do with instruction, yet has much to do with that higher knowledge of which Plato spoke. The English people do not seem to love the higher theatre, love the spirit of the theatre, as have done the citizens of some other lands. They are content to witness certain plays ; they follow great (and mediocre) actors ; but of the theatre as a force, as an entity independent of playwright and actor, as a power embracing many arts, they have no conception. Their theatre is imaginatively and mentally inert because they, as a nation, do not demand a theatre that shall be alive and

pulsating with energy. A Shakespeare playhouse
at Stratford based partly on the generosity of
others, a Shakespeare theatre in London tucked
away in Waterloo Road, a National Shakespeare
Theatre which is merely a dream—these, even
in spite of lip-worship devoted to him who is
styled " The Bard," are their records.

Maybe there are signs of an awakening ; perhaps the old prejudices will disappear ; but, until
they do disappear, we can hope for little from the
English stage. The drama as such has flourished,
and no doubt will continue so to flourish, but that
is not the theatre. Until in England audiences
come to realize that the play is only an excuse for
the theatre, that the total impression made upon
an audience by a particular performance depends
upon much more than the spoken word, and that
the theatre is something more than a place either
of amusement or of oratory, we shall not be able
to discover on the English stage any true realiza-
tion of richer ideals in theatric terms.

That the fault lies, not in the stars, but in the
spectators themselves is unquestionably true ; yet
external conditions have not been without their
influence in creating the present-day world of the
playhouse. One such, which naturally affects all
countries, is the fact that new ideals in literary
expression have the tendency to make modern
artists despise dramatic expression. By far the
most pronounced and influential artistic movement of our times has been that which introduced
the sphere of the subconscious. The novel, which

in the hands of Fielding and Scott and Dickens had dealt either with exciting incident or with boldly outlined personalities, at once has broadened and narrowed its scope. Instead of epically covering whole decades and presenting rich galleries of fictional types, it has concentrated on limited periods and striven, by excessive attention to minute detail, to delve far into the recesses of the human soul. James Joyce's *Ulysses*, the extreme example of this style, is yet thoroughly representative. The stream of consciousness, narrated through the course of several hundred pages, brings before us a realm hitherto entirely neglected by the literary artists. Into this realm the drama may hardly enter. Attempts have been made, no doubt, but the limited extent of a theatrical performance and the fundamentally objective approach demanded of the playwright, deny to it the opportunities offered to narrative fiction. The theatre will always be compelled to subsist on bold effects; always will the stage call for physical action; the characters, whatever subtlety be introduced, must always be delineated in a manner alien to that which has created such a revolution in the modern novel. There can be no doubt that an appreciation of these limitations has restrained many modern men of letters from experimenting in dramatic form. In the nineties and early nineteen hundreds the play seemed that kind of expression most suited to the ideals of the period; hence Jones and Pinero, Wilde and Shaw, Barrie and Galsworthy, all turned to the theatre;

and the theatre itself, as we have seen, won a position which it had not had since the days of Elizabeth. Now, this same theatre makes less of an appeal to the artists, and perhaps attracts less the body of instructed and sensitive opinion by whose influence it might continue to develop.

Such facts had best be accepted frankly ; but, in accepting them, we may suggest that, even with the progress of new ideals in art, there will still be room for the stage. Our enthusiasm for deeply searching novels which flow on monotonously as the Danube should not blind us to the fact that the theatre, by its more stormy methods, may create an imaginative excitement as worthy our æsthetic esteem, that through the combined visual and aural appeal of the playhouse something may be achieved inachievable in other forms of art. At the same time, the theatre itself must take into account the progress in conception displayed by its sister arts ; and here again we return to the old question of realism. The realistic method is precisely that most calculated to antagonize those on whom the mantle of the new dispensation has fallen, that realism being based essentially upon a purely objective approach. If the theatre were to throw that aside, become what gives it greatest scope and embrace once more the conventionalism on which previously it has thrived, we might again discover in it that thrilling sense of wonder and extraordinary sureness of touch whence came a Sophocles and a Shakespeare, an Athenian and an Elizabethan stage.

More directly affecting the English playhouse is the change in theatrical organization which has led to the development of the " commercial " stages and the consequent disappearance of the repertory system. In one sense, all theatres have been, and are, commercial ; but no age has produced such conditions as prevail in London at present, where practically all the playhouses, instead of being owned by those in control of their operation, are let and sub-let by men who, save in so far as they are in possession of the buildings themselves, have no interest in the art of the stage. To this is due, partly at least, the high costs of theatrical production and the resultant prices of admission which make theatre-going inordinately more expensive than film-going for those in the stalls and circle, and even considerably more for those who are willing to deny themselves the plush-covered armchairs of the cinema and accept the discomforts of the theatre's upper-circle and gallery. That this is unfortunate and that it materially contributes towards preventing the theatre from competing equally with the cinema is most assuredly true ; yet we cannot escape from the reflection that playhouse finances have never been in a good state in any period, and that there were illiterate Philip Henslowes who controlled and hindered the actors even in Shakespeare's time.

Of greater seriousness, perhaps, is the fact that the new conditions have utterly destroyed the old stock company system and rendered the traditional repertory unknown. In London only two theatres

—The Old Vic and Sadler's Wells—carry on anything approaching the methods in common operation at Drury Lane and Covent Garden during the early part of the nineteenth century. The disappearance of the stock company (both in London and in the various provincial centres) was due to a number of thoroughly understandable causes. For London, the rapid increase of the population, and hence of the play-going public, was largely responsible, and, in noting this, we must remember that the inventiveness of the age had provided new means of conveyance which converted what had hitherto been outlying villages into portions of the metropolis. In 1800 a trip from Richmond to see a play would have been well-nigh unthinkable ; by the end of the century it had become normal practice. The consequence was that the long run established itself. During the seventeenth century eight or nine consecutive performances of a new play was such a startling event that the publishers of the text deemed it fitting to advertise the wonder on the title-page of their edition. The year 1728 set a new record by giving a whole month to *The Beggar's Opera*, and, as has been noted, the vogue of the pantomime succeeded in providing even longer runs for at least the subsidiary elements in the theatre's repertoire. Only in the nineteenth century, however, do we find the practice of presenting a tragedy or a comedy for as long as it will draw spectators, and that practice clearly depends on the increase in the potential audience. Once introduced, it rendered the old stock company useless. When the evening's bill was constantly changing, obviously a theatre had to maintain a salaried set of performers, each carefully chosen for his " line of business," so that in concert they might attempt almost any play, new or ancient, tragedy or comedy, that might be called for. The development of the long run, coupled with the growing desire for greater realism which substituted individual treatment of parts for type treatment, made it advantageous to gather a special company together for any given play. A playwright no longer created his characters with the Drury Lane or Covent Garden performers in his mind's eye, and a manager no longer read his scripts with the thought of particular actors in his employ ; each had virtually the whole range of the histrionic profession to draw from.

Similar conditions destroyed the local stock troupes. Of old, each large town had its Theatre Royal and its own company ; there a varied repertoire was presented, consisting partly of classic dramas and partly of recent London successes. Occasionally the performances were varied by the calling in for a few evenings of some visiting " star "—a Mrs. Siddons or an Edmund Kean— who, because the stock companies were all built up to a like plan and because the repertoires were standard, was able to take his or her part in a performance without more than a single rehearsal. Besides such stock companies were those engaged on various circuits, carrying the theatre to smaller centres which could not support a permanent troupe, and those, too, were fashioned along similar lines.

With the coming of the railway the independence of the local stock companies was destroyed. London managers found that they could reap a double profit by gathering a second, a third, even a fourth troupe, these troupes being sent on tour throughout the country, playing for an entire week in the larger centres and using smaller places for " one-night stands." The esteem connected with the London success went with them ; the public preferred to see their performances rather than those of the familiar stock company ; and the manager of the local Theatre Royal soon found that he could do a more profitable business by letting his house to those touring bands than by maintaining his own set of actors. One by one, therefore, the provincial companies disappeared, and the touring system was established.

The old conditions brought with them certain disadvantages—among them the chief being that the " lines of business " tended towards a stereotyping of dramatic parts—but the advantages were numerous. The system provided ample opportunity to the young apprentice player. He could obtain, without too much difficulty, a provincial engagement, apply himself there to a score of rôles during the course of a season and have the chance of studying the varied methods of trained performers. Having received his experience thus, he might then look forward to a London position where once more he might expect rich variety in the parts allotted to him. In addition to this, the spectators always had kept before them the principal riches of dramatic literature. Shakespeare's plays were constantly being performed, and, along with these, scores of plays by other dramatists which, by their merits, had become "stock pieces." The theatres, then, were much more than places where new tragedies and comedies might be produced ; they were living dramatic libraries where Shakespeare and Jonson, Vanbrugh and Farquhar, Colman and Murphy, were periodically displayed.

The decay of the stock company and the establishment of the long run utterly destroyed this repertoire. Shakespeare might still be presented (in long-run fashion) by an Irving or a Tree : occasional " revivals " there might be of older plays : but the regular acquaintanceship with England's dramatic heritage had gone. Contemporaries were not without an awareness of the needs of the time. From 1870 onwards we find appeals for a " Dramatic Academy " where young players might receive their training, and these appeals eventually found material expression in the foundation of The Royal Academy of Dramatic Art. Suddenly, too, men realized that, whereas France and Germany had numbers of national and municipal theatres, England had none. During the seventies, therefore, appeals for an Academy were coupled with appeals for a National Theatre, where the best of the older plays might be preserved; this, however, has not met with any success. All that was accomplished was the drawing of attention to the need and the establishment of a few organizations designed in part at least to meet it. The Stage Society (and, for a time, The Phœnix Society) periodically brought sixteenth and seventeenth century plays before the attention of the public, thus carrying out the work projected many years before by The Dramatic Students, an organization active in 1886. The statement of their aims (presented in *The Saturday Review of Literature*) succinctly indicates the change that had come over the theatrical world in London :

The Dramatic Students are a society of young professional actors, who, finding that the long runs now common in successful plays give them scant occasion to gain variety of skill in their art, have determined to bring out, in single morning performances, the less known masterpieces of English dramatic literature. They eschew such plays as are included in the ordinary repertory. . . . We follow their efforts with great interest, for we believe that these form the nucleus of a very wholesome revival of interest in the best theatrical writing. . . . By-and-by this seed will, we do not doubt, bear fruit, and the public will insist on seeing more of these interesting pieces, and on seeing them repeated. It is a sheer absurdity that our seventeenth-century dramatic literature should be without dispute one of the richest ornaments of our language and yet that none of it, except three or four plays of Shakespeare's, should ever be seen, even for a moment on the stage.

The allusion here to " morning performances " reminds us that, owing to the same new conditions, the matinée came into being also about this time. Originally it was designed to serve two purposes— to give an opportunity for the seeing of older plays which otherwise would have been forgotten, and to provide a means whereby younger authors might have their works tried out. For it is not to be forgotten that the dramatists were suffering like the rest. During the reign of the dramatic monopoly there may have been complaints levelled by disappointed playwrights at callous managers, but, since the company was there and little new scenery had to be specially prepared, it was fairly easy for an inexperienced author to get his comedy or tragedy put on the boards. If failure resulted, after all that failure would result in no more than the loss of two or three nights' play. Now, however, things were different. Before a manager accepted a piece for production he naturally hesitated, for he had to think of leasing a theatre he did not own, of engaging a special company, of commissioning special scenery. His costs were considerable, and unless the play were to run at least a few months he would lose a vast amount of capital. The tendency, as may readily be imagined, was for these managers to turn to established playwrights, already noted for their successes, and ignore the men whose efforts had not been tried. During this period we hear much of the vicious " dramatic ring." In the matinée, then, a means of escape was found, although this, too, soon was taken away. So great had the potential audience become that managers discovered playgoers willing to attend, not merely the regular six evening shows, but a couple of afternoon performances as well. The matinée, therefore, simply became incorporated in the regular working playhouse hours.

Since 1900 two movements have served to do something both to alleviate this set of conditions and to provide some hope for the future. The first of these is the growth of the repertory theatre. Not exceedingly healthy, perhaps, this growth, and usually needing ample support : yet, because it flourishes at all, demanding our attention and esteem. The typical repertory theatre of to-day is, in one respect, to be regarded as the modern representative of the old stock company, but during the passage of years that stock company has suffered a sea change. Based on a similar foundation, with a permanent staff and a salaried group of performers, presenting a series of plays with only limited runs throughout the course of a season, the repertory playhouse of to-day yet has aims beyond those embraced by the members of the old Theatres Royal. It strives to encourage young talent, and it aims at regularly reviving earlier plays which have not recently been seen on the boards. Compelled often it may be to put on a version of London's latest farcical success, but it invariably does so with many regrets and intellectual apologies.

Starting in 1903 with Miss Horniman's Abbey Theatre in Dublin, where a more than common effort was made to encourage and to stimulate local talent, the movement has spread markedly during the course of thirty years. Miss Horniman was also responsible for the Manchester Repertory at the Gaiety in 1908. A Liverpool Repertory directed by Basil Dean came in 1911 ; in 1913 Barry Jackson organized the Repertory at Birmingham. At a dozen centres similar movements were set on foot, and to-day there are over thirty professional repertory companies, extending from old-established theatres such as Birmingham possesses and recently vitalized groups like William Armstrong's Liverpool Playhouse down to Little Theatres operating more precariously, and to itinerant organizations of the type of the Masque Theatre or the Jevon Brandon-Thomas Players, both of which, by performing in large theatres at low prices, are ably competing with the cinema in the North. To keep these alive may often prove difficult, and one must recognize that so far London has set its face against things of the kind. Even Granville Barker's effort at the Court, brilliant as his productions must have been, did not result in any real profit. Occasional repertory seasons have been tried, but they were largely the work of keen enthusiasts and drew but small audiences. The Old Vic and Sadler's Wells gain good houses, yet they could not subsist without support from without. Sydney Carroll's open-air theatre in Regent's Park, of course, thrives; we might not, however, in spite of the interesting experiments made there and the excellence of work exhibited, expect any equivalent success were the same performances given in a regular winter season on an ordinary stage.

Whatever the difficulties and however futile has hitherto been the endeavour to establish repertory in the West End of London, the fact that the number of such theatres throughout the country has increased fourfold from the original ten of 1913 yet indicates that there is a widespread, general and wholesome interest in the theatre, and that real efforts are being made to discover some means of mitigating the evil effects attendant upon modern playhouse conditions. In accepting this statement, however, it is important that we should not regard the repertories as an ideal with which to replace interest in the current " commercial " houses. That is a tendency on the part of many enthusiasts who believe that, if the serious theatre is to survive in England, the commercial organizations must be destroyed and the repertory reign. Tempting though this view may be, on examination it must be proved, because false alike to the age's need and to the fundamental spirit of the theatre, essentially untenable. The theatre always must be coloured by and accept its principles from the social

conditions of its time. To look back with longing
eyes towards the antique stock companies were
ridiculous ; these days are done with. Modern
surroundings could give them no room for life.
That the local repertory has done, is doing, and
is likely to continue doing, excellent work, that
it deserves every support which we can give it, that
it has shown itself indeed a necessary element in
the modern theatre-world—all this we may readily
agree, but we shall by no means be justified in
proceeding to the assumption that in the repertory
system lies the sole hope of theatrical progress.
Not only is commercialism an integral part of
stage enterprise, but we have always found drama
flourishing, not in local centres, but in some large
metropolis—a Periclean Athens, an Elizabethan
or Victorian London, a Paris of Louis Quatorze.

With the repertory theatre must be associated
the vast amateur movement which has become so
characteristic a product of the present day. In
ancient times aristocratic amateurs amused themselves and bored their guests by the performance
of dramas either in large halls or in specially
constructed private theatres ; and even the
eighteenth century had its plebeian " spouting
clubs," which provided satirical merriment for
Arthur Murphy. The modern amateur organizations, however, differ markedly from those of the
past ; like the repertory theatres, they too have
been transformed. Instead of habitually playing
Ici on parle français, they experiment in the most
extreme of dramatic forms, and at least a dozen

of them have developed so ambitious an organization that they might almost be classed among the repertory theatres. The growth and success of The British Drama League and of The Scottish Community Drama Association is but an index of their widespread activity. There may be many who share Julian Huxley's horror of amateur theatricals, and imagine with him that if they were turned into dictators one of their first decrees would be devoted to forbidding the amateur production of plays, and it is manifestly absurd to profess, as some do, that the best, the truest, and the most " sincere " acting is to be found among the ranks of the amateurs. On the other hand, all this activity is to the good. Not only do the amateurs often present plays which otherwise would remain nothing but printed texts, they assist in building up an audience for the professional theatre. That possibly is their greatest service to the drama as a whole, for from their own efforts they are likely to bring a more informed and certainly a more eager appreciation to the worthier efforts of commercial managers.

Two things, however, seem lacking. The British Drama League has succeeded in coordinating the work of the many hundred scattered producing societies, but that co-ordination is for the most part an external association. A few groups have created for themselves a definite policy ; some of the verse-speaking choirs, for example, deliberately set for their aim the building up of better methods in the stage delivery of poetic forms and the encouragement of modern poetic drama such as Gordon Bottomley is producing. In general, however, the amateur society has no object of this kind ; it simply chooses the plays which seem best fitted for interpretation by its members, and so lives a purposeless existence from performance to performance. What is required is a driving impulse of the sort which informs the activities of the numerous left-wing groups in America. The propaganda theatre we may condemn in theory, but there can be no doubt that the enthusiasm engendered in the presentation of such plays provides an inner coordination and a fundamental sense of purpose lacking in the average amateur society.

The second thing wanting is a closer link between the amateur and the professional stages, and here once more the example of America may be adduced. Many of the more important American universities bring dramatic work within the scope of the college curriculum, and this dramatic work often assumes a wholly or largely professional scope. At Yale University, for example, the aim is set of providing fully professional training in all branches of theatrical art for students who have already had the benefit of a college education and who thus possess an adequate intellectual background. The young dramatist is there given an opportunity of seeing his plays put upon the stage ; the scene designer experiments with more than paper and pencil ; the producer learns by practical experience with actors. By this means, not only is an opportunity offered to those who feel the call of the theatre, but the theatre itself is being fed by men and women who combine the advantages of a broad cultural training with the most exact professional instruction. Students graduating thence proceed to the commercial theatres and serve there in various capacities, while others undertake the directing of little theatres throughout the country. This is not to say that in America the professional and little theatres form one entity, or even that their interests are closely allied ; in many instances, indeed, the very reverse is true, and the former look with jealous eyes on the success of the latter. Nevertheless, the links are more evident than in England. While numbers of the smaller community theatres are little but social clubs, and desultorily present unambitious performances, others maintain high standards of artistic excellence and apply professional principles to the arrangements for their productions. Moreover, among them are several which either rise beyond the amateur altogether or else aid in fusing the two. The Pasadena Community Playhouse is doing something of fundamental importance for the theatre as a whole, and justly famous is the Cleveland Playhouse which, professionally directed and maintaining a regular company of salaried actors, can work in intimate relationship with the dramatic department of the city's university. Both amateur and professional in its organization, at once a place of artistic achievement and a training ground, these theatres provide an atmosphere which seems to be lacking in England.

Perhaps in time something approaching this will gradually evolve itself in England too ; unquestionably such a development is much to be desired. Even as matters stand, the recent rise of the amateurs and the closely associated increase in the number of repertory playhouses testify to a growing, a real and an appreciative interest in the drama which well may mark the beginnings of a fresh rebirth of enthusiasm for the theatre. To be truly vital, however, that enthusiasm must be genuinely for the theatre, and therefore for all that the theatre implies ; it must be gifted with a sense of purpose at present wanting ; and it must have an excitingly arresting aim. The growth of the amateur societies suggests that potentially the vigour and the impulse are there ; but vigour of the kind so far displayed is not enough. Several hundred productions extending from the positively bad through the vast mediocre to the rare nearly good, the holding of conferences and the arranging of summer schools with summary instruction in drama, acting and production methods—all these unquestionably have their value, but that value must be strictly limited by reason of the inherent conditions. That we need not despair of the theatre in England seems certain ; that these new things promise hope for the future seems equally sure ; but before we may dream of seeing a renewed passion for the stage of the kind that animated the reigns of Elizabeth and of Victoria, more must be realized, and still more must be created in the spirit of the ideal. A clearer understanding is demanded of what the theatre has meant to earlier generations, of the changes in society to which it has had to adjust itself, and of those things which might be apt to stir it again to feverish activity.

" Time is : Time was : Time is past " were the mysterious sentences spoken by Friar Bacon's brazen head. The theatre, although it seems a form of art whose expression lives only in the fleeting moment, has its roots deep buried in the past, and it anticipates a new flowering to-morrow. Neither the creation of a rootless artificial bloom nor the snipping of a flower in the hope that for a time it may be preserved can equal that vital strength which comes alone from the budding and bursting of fresh petals. Time makes its demands of us if we desire a theatre that shall live and signify to those of our age what so often it has signified to earlier generations.

NOTES ON SOME OF THE PRINCIPAL LONDON THEATRES
1576–1935

[Provincial theatres are not included in this list, and only some of the more important suburban houses find mention. Before 1576 there were no permanent theatres in England, if we except the Roman playhouse at Verulamium (St. Albans) and the Cornish "rounds." Two of these "rounds" are still to be seen, at St. Just and at Perranzabuloe, near Perranporth. The latter is the more interesting, and displays clearly the earthen walls of the ancient amphitheatre.]

ELIZABETHAN THEATRES

The professional companies first used various London inn-yards, notably those of the *Bell*, the *Cross Keys* (both in Gracechurch Street), the *Bull* (in Bishopsgate Street), the *Bell Savage* (in Ludgate), and the *Boar's Head* (in Whitechapel Street). These were still occasionally utilized even after the regular houses of entertainment had been erected.

The Theatre, in Finsbury Field, Shoreditch. Erected in 1576 by James Burbage, and used by various companies until in 1598 it was pulled down, the timber being used for building *The Globe*.

The Curtain, in Finsbury Field. Erected about 1577. Used by various companies, notably by the Lord Chamberlain's men (*c*. 1597–1599). It was in existence as late as 1627.

Blackfriars (the first theatre), in the buildings of the old monastery. Erected by Richard Farrant in 1576. Used by the Children of Windsor and of the Chapel Royal. The theatre was closed in 1584.

St. Paul's. The boys of St. Paul's were performing in a theatre situated near the Cathedral in 1578. Little is known of their playhouse.

Newington Butts. Erected before 1580. Used by various companies, including the joint Admiral's and Chamberlain's in 1594. It was no doubt torn down shortly after this date.

The Rose, in Southwark. Erected in 1587. Strange's men occupied it in 1592, Sussex' in 1593, Admiral's in 1594. It was pulled down about 1605.

The Swan, in Paris Garden. Erected 1595. Used by various companies. It seems to have ceased to be a theatre in 1621.

Blackfriars (the second theatre). Erected by Burbage in 1596. Used by Children's companies until, in 1608, it became the winter headquarters of the King's men until the shutting of the theatres in 1642. It was destroyed in 1655.

The Globe, in Southwark. Erected in 1599 by the Lord Chamberlain's men, the timber of *The Theatre* being used for its construction. Used by the Lord Chamberlain's (King's) men until it was burned in 1613. A second *Globe* theatre was opened in 1614 by the same company and was utilized till 1642. It was pulled down in 1644.

The Fortune, near Golding Lane. Erected in 1600. Used by the Admiral's men and by various later companies until 1621, when it was burned down. A new *Fortune* was opened in 1623, and used by the Palsgrave's men and others until 1642. It seems to have been employed occasionally during the Commonwealth period, but was pulled down about 1661.

The Red Bull, in Clerkenwell. Erected about 1605,

and used by various companies until 1642. It had a reputation for rant and bombast. It was also utilized after the Restoration until 1663.

Whitefriars, below Fleet Street. Erected about 1605 for the Children of His Majesty's Revels, but given over in 1614.

The Hope, in Southwark. Erected in 1613. Used by various companies until 1616. It was utilized as a Bear Garden after 1660.

The Phœnix, or *Cockpit-in-Court*, in Drury Lane. This, the first theatre in Drury Lane, was erected in 1617 by William Beeston and was used into the period of the Restoration.

Salisbury Court, sometimes called the *Whitefriars*. Erected in 1629. It was still in existence in the early years of the Restoration period.

The Cockpit-in-Court, in Whitehall. Used for plays from about 1604. A new building was erected in 1632. Performances were given here in the Restoration period, when it was materially reconstructed.

RESTORATION

Before the erection of new theatres in this period, several old theatres were made use of—notably *The Red Bull*, *The Cockpit*, and *Salisbury Court*.

Theatre Royal, in Vere Street. Converted from Gibbon's Tennis Court in 1660 and used by the King's men until 1663.

Lincoln's Inn Fields. Opened by D'Avenant for the Duke's men in 1661. It was used by them until 1671, and was later (in 1695) occupied by Betterton's seceding actors. In the eighteenth century it was one of the two patent theatres, its rights passing on to *Covent Garden*.

Theatre Royal, in Bridges Street. Opened in 1663 by

the King's men and used by them until it was burned to the ground in 1672.

The Hall Theatre, in Whitehall. Constructed as a theatre in 1665.

The Duke's Theatre, in Dorset Garden. Opened in 1671 by the Duke's men and used by them till the Union of the Companies in 1682. It was a very large theatre, and later was abandoned except for the production of spectacular pieces.

Theatre Royal, in Drury Lane. Opened in 1674 by the King's men. From 1682 to 1695 it was occupied by the United Companies of the King's men and the Duke's men. Altered slightly by Rich at the end of the century, *Drury Lane* remained the chief theatre in London until it was abandoned in 1791.

EIGHTEENTH CENTURY

Drury Lane, as we have seen, was in occupation till 1791 ; the old theatre in *Lincoln's Inn Fields* was used by Betterton up to 1705 ; and occasional performances were given in *Dorset Garden* previous to its demolishment in 1709.

The Haymarket, originally called *The Queen's Theatre*, later *The Opera House* and *King's Theatre*. Erected by Vanbrugh and Congreve in 1705. This was used for plays in the early years of the century, but soon became established as the home of Italian opera in England. It was the scene of Händel's chief activities. The building was completely destroyed by fire in 1789, but a new *King's Theatre* was opened the following year. In 1867 (when it was known as *Her Majesty's*) this second structure was also gutted by fire.

Lincoln's Inn Fields, known as the new or little theatre. Opened in 1714 by John Rich and used for plays (both in English and in French) until the building of *Covent Garden*. From 1732 to 1737 it was occupied by various minor companies, and after the Licensing Act continued its activities with pantomimes and musical plays.

The Haymarket ; the Little Theatre, or *The French Theatre.* Opened in 1720 with performances by a French company. Its most notable early tenancy was that of Henry Fielding (1735–1737).

Goodman's Fields. In 1729 Giffard opened the first theatre in Leman Street. This was silenced in 1730, but a second *Goodman's Fields Theatre,* in Ayliffe Street, was opened in 1731. Irregular performances were given in it up to 1746, and here David Garrick made his first appearance in London.

Covent Garden. Opened in 1732 by John Rich, who brought to it the Lincoln's Inn Fields actors. Altered in 1782 and enlarged in 1792, it remained one of the two Patent theatres until it was destroyed by fire in 1808.

Sadler's Wells. At this place of entertainment various pantomimic and musical pieces were given from about 1740. The fabric of the theatre built there in 1765 endured till 1931. Notable for spectacular, pantomimic, and melodramatic pieces in the early nineteenth century, it achieved sudden fame through the activities of Samuel Phelps, who produced here, from 1844 to 1862, his famous series of revivals. After being abandoned for a number of years, it has now once more sprung into prominence through its purchase by the *Old Vic.*

The Haymarket ; Theatre Royal. Opened in 1766 by Samuel Foote, who had obtained a licence to present plays during the summer. The new *Theatre Royal* stood on the site of the former *Little Theatre.* It continued its career until in 1825 the present *Theatre Royal* took its place (as reconstructed in 1880).

The Royalty, in Wellclose Square, Goodman's Fields.

Erected by John Palmer in 1787. Failing to obtain a licence for plays, Palmer presented mimic entertainments here. In 1810 it was known as *The East London Theatre*. Fire destroyed it in 1826.

The Pantheon, in Oxford Street. Opened as an opera house in 1790, but gutted by fire in 1792. The portico still remains as the front of Gilbey's wine store.

Drury Lane. A new *Drury Lane* was opened in 1794 and destroyed by fire in 1809.

Nineteenth Century

Besides *Drury Lane, Covent Garden*, the two theatres in the *Haymarket* and *Sadler's Wells*, the nineteenth century inherited from the eighteenth a number of minor houses, notably *The Royal Circus*, which became *The Surrey*, and *Astley's Amphitheatre*.

Astley's, near Westminster Bridge. Built on the site of an older ring (1795) in 1804. Its most famous period was between 1830 and 1841, when Ducrow was manager. Later it was taken over by " Sangers'." Finally destroyed to make room for Westminster Bridge Road.

The Adelphi, in the Strand. First called *The Sans Pareil*. Opened in 1806 for music and dancing under Charles Dibdin. Renamed *The Adelphi* in 1819, it was rebuilt in 1858. Success came to it under the managements of William Farren, Alfred Wigan, and William Terriss, the last of whom made it the home of " Adelphi drama." Rebuilt in 1901 as *The Century*, it was for some time the headquarters of Oscar Asche.

The Olympic, in Wych Street, Strand. Opened as *The Olympic Pavilion* by Philip Astley in 1804 for " Public Music and Dancing." In 1809 it was granted a licence for burlettas. In 1831 Madame Vestris took control and popularized extravaganza there. The

theatre was burned to the ground in 1849, and a new
Olympic, finally closed in 1899, was opened in 1850.

The Sans Souci, in Leicester Place.   This house of
entertainment had been opened by Dibdin in the
preceding century.   Frederick Schirmer produced
" Musical and Dramatic Interludes in the German
Language " there in 1805.   In 1806 it attempted to
make itself a dramatic academy under the name of
The Academic Theatre (licensed for " Plays and Entertainments performed by Children under 17 Years of
Age and for Music and Dancing ").   Vaudeville entertainments were being given there in 1833.

Argyll Rooms, Argyll Street.   The dramatic academy
run by F. Greville moved here from *The Sans Souci* in
1807.   Between 1819 and 1823 several French plays
were performed in this " theatre."

Covent Garden.   The new *Covent Garden* was opened
in 1809.   Here Charles Kemble, Edmund Kean, and
Macready won fame.   By 1847, however, the theatre
was given over to Italian opera.   After the fire of 1856
the present *Covent Garden Opera House* was opened in
1858.

The Lyceum, in the Strand.   In a building originally
erected in 1765 as an exhibition room and used for
concerts from 1794, S. J. Arnold, in 1809, started *The
English Opera House, Lyceum*.   Here the *Drury Lane*
actors appeared after the destruction of their theatre
in 1809.   A new theatre was opened in 1816 and
granted a licence for four months each year till it was
destroyed by fire in 1830.   Another *Lyceum* was
erected in 1834 and managed by the Keeleys from
1844 to 1847, by Madame Vestris and Charles Mathews
from 1847 to 1855, and by Henry Irving from 1878 to
1902.

The Queen's, off Tottenham Court Road.   Altered
(in 1809) from *The King's Concert Rooms* (built in 1790)
and first known as *The Regency*.   *The Queen's Theatre*

had many aliases, the most famous being *The Prince of Wales's*. It achieved fame under the management of Squire Bancroft and Marie Wilton (1865–1879). It was demolished in 1882. On its site stands the present *Scala Theatre* (1904).

The Surrey, in Waterloo Road. Opened in 1811 in the building formerly known as *The Royal Circus*. It became famous for a special type of melodrama and flourished until the fire of 1865. It was rebuilt in 1867.

Drury Lane. The new *Theatre Royal* was opened, under the management of a committee of which Byron was a member, in 1812. With various alterations, this stands to the present day. Edmund Kean made his historic appearance there in 1814. Elliston assumed the management in 1819, and Alfred Bunn took command of both the patent theatres in the thirties. Augustus Harris and Arthur Collins made it fairly prosperous by the production of rich spectacles.

The Royal Coburg, in Waterloo Road. Opened in 1818. In its early days it specialized in melodrama, but tended more and more towards the " legitimate " drama. The name *Victoria* dates from 1833, and it is now officially known as *The Old Vic*, having been made into a home for Shakespeare by Miss Lilian Bayliss.

The Theatre Royal, Haymarket. Part of the present building dates from 1825 ; it was rebuilt in 1880. The most important early managements were those of Benjamin Webster (1835–1853) and J. B. Buckstone (1853–1876). The Bancrofts moved there in 1879, and in 1885 Beerbohm Tree took control. Frederick Harrison and Cyril Maude from 1896 set a high standard in production.

The Pavilion, in Whitechapel Road. Opened in 1829 and burned in 1856, this house was once famous for its melodrama. The present building has become

The Interior of the Lyric Theatre, Hammersmith.
From a painting by George Sheringham, showing a performance of
The Duenna.

equally noted as the home of Yiddish drama in the East End.

The Garrick, in Leman Street, Whitechapel. Opened in 1830 on the site of the old *Goodman's Fields* house. This was burned in 1846. Rebuilt a few years later, it persisted on to the seventies.

The Princess's, in Oxford Street. In 1830 entertainments were being given here. It was called *The Queen's* in 1834, *The Court* in 1836, and *The Royal Princess's* in 1840, when it was rebuilt. Charles Kean's famous revivals were presented there between 1850 and 1862 ; Wilson Barrett was manager from 1881 to 1889. The theatre was abandoned in 1902.

The Strand. Opened as a theatre in 1830, and at one time famous for its burlesques. From 1833 to 1835 it was licensed for performances by Miss Kelly, and received a " burletta " licence in 1835 (issued to L. B. Rayner and Captain Bell). Various managements took control, its most famous days being in the sixties with H. J. Byron's travesties and extravaganzas. It was destroyed to make room for the Aldwych Tube Station.

The City, in Milton Street, Cripplegate. This house was one of the more respectable " minors " between 1831 and 1836, when it was demolished.

The Orange Street Theatre, in King's Road, Chelsea. Opened in 1831, but soon abandoned.

The Albion, in Windmill Street, Haymarket. This was opened about 1832, renamed *The New Queen's* (1833), and closed in 1836.

King's Cross. Opened in 1832, and known by a variety of names—*The Clarence, The New Lyceum, The Regent, The Argyll,* and *The Cabinet.*

The New Royal Sussex, in Church Street, Edgeware Road. Opened in 1832 and variously known as *The Pavilion, The Royal Pavilion, The Portman,* and *The Royal Marylebone.* Rebuilt in 1864, it was named

The Royal Alfred in 1868 and *The West London* in 1893.

The Westminster, in Tothill Street.   Opened in 1832, and abandoned in 1835.

The Grecian, in Shepherdess Walk.   Opened in 1832 by T. Rouse and taken over by George Conquest in 1851.   Also known as *The Royal Eagle Saloon*.

The Globe, in Blackfriars Road.   This was used as a theatre in 1833, but by 1838 had been turned into a music hall.

The Royal Borough, in Tooley Street.   Used as a theatre between 1834 and 1836.

The Royal Kent, in Kensington High Street.   Opened in 1834 and closed in 1840.   Also called *The Kensington*.

The Royal Standard, in Shoreditch.   Opened in 1835, remodelled in 1845, and burned in 1866.   A new house was opened in 1868.

St. James's, in King Street, St. James's.   Opened in 1835 by J. Braham and used mainly by French companies in its early years.   In 1840 Braham changed its name to *The Prince's* and took out a licence for the production of German operas.   The theatre had little success until it was taken over by the Kendals in 1879. In 1891 George Alexander became its manager.

The City of London, near Bishopsgate Station. Opened in 1835 and eventually closed in 1868.

The Manor House, in King's Row, Chelsea.   Used in 1837.

The New Royalty, in Dean Street, Soho.   Built in 1840 by Miss Kelly.   It achieved little success until after its reconstruction in 1861, when it won fame for burlesques.   In 1883 the theatre was again reconstructed under the management of Kate Santley, and finally remodelled in 1905.

The Britannia, Hoxton.   From 1841 to 1899 famous for its " minor " drama.   It was under one management for half a century, Mrs. Sarah Lane, widow of the original owner, having control of it from 1849 to 1899.

The East London, Whitechapel. Opened in 1844, rebuilt in 1867, and burned in 1870. A new theatre on the old site was for years a home of Yiddish drama, but this also was destroyed by fire.

St. Martin's Hall. Opened in 1855 by German Reed.

The Gallery of Illustration, in Waterloo Place. Opened in 1856 by German Reed.

The London Pavilion. Opened in 1861, remodelled in 1885 and 1918.

The Holborn. Opened in 1866. Variously known as *The Duke's*, *The Curtain*, *The Mirror.* It was destroyed in 1880.

St. George's Hall, in Langham Place. Opened in 1867 by German Reed and Corney Grain. Renamed *The Matinée* in 1897.

The Queen's, in Longacre. Opened in 1867, on the site of *St. Martin's Hall* (1855). This theatre had a fairly distinguished career under Henry Labouchere. It was abandoned in 1866.

The Gaiety. Opened in 1868 by John Hollingshead, and demolished in 1903. A new *Gaiety* was opened in 1903. George Edwardes became manager in 1886. Burlesque and musical comedy have been its staple fare.

The Globe, in Newcastle Street. Opened in 1868 and abandoned in 1902.

The Charing Cross Theatre, in King William Street, Strand. Originally built as *The Polygraphic Hall.* Opened as a theatre in 1869, more famous as *The Folly* (1876) and as *Toole's* (1882). It was demolished in 1896. J. L. Toole owned and managed it from 1879 to 1895.

The Vaudeville. Opened in 1870, reconstructed in 1891 and 1925. Managed by David James and

Thomas Thorne for several years, and later by A. and S. Gatti.

The Opera Comique, in the Strand.   Opened in 1870. For some time the home of the Gilbert and Sullivan opera.   It was demolished in 1897.

The Grand, Islington.   Opened as a theatre in 1870. It was burned in 1882, and a new playhouse, opened in 1883, was similarly burned in 1887.   A third, opened in 1888, was burned in 1900.

The Alhambra, in Leicester Square.   This house started as a " Panopticon " in 1854 ;   it became a " music hall " in 1853 and a " theatre " in 1871. Reconstructed in 1883, it won considerable success by its variety shows.

The Court, Chelsea.   Opened in 1871 as *The New Chelsea Theatre.*   This house was pulled down in 1887, but a new theatre on the same site was opened in 1888. Famous early managers were Marie Wilton and John Hare.   During the nineties it housed several " advanced " performances by the Stage Society and the Independent Theatre.   The Granville-Barker-Vedrenne management brought it distinction, as did the later management of Sir Barry Jackson.

The Park Theatre, Camden Town, also known as *The Alexandra.*   Opened in 1871 and destroyed by fire in 1881.

The Elephant and Castle, in New Kent Road. Opened in 1872, remodelled in 1882 and 1902.

Crystal Palace.   Opened in 1874.

The Criterion.   Opened in 1874, reconstructed in 1884 and 1903.   It had little success until Charles Wyndham joined Alexander Henderson in management (1875).   This lasted till 1899.

The Imperial, Westminster.   Opened in 1876 as *The Aquarium Theatre,* and renamed *The Imperial* in 1879. It was reconstructed by Mrs. Langtry in 1901, but it passed out of existence a few years later.

The Comedy. Opened in 1881. It has had a distinguished career under a variety of managements.

The Savoy. Opened in 1881, and for long the home of the Gilbert and Sullivan opera. In 1907 Granville-Barker and Vedrenne transferred to this theatre from *The Court.*

The Avenue. Opened in 1882, and partially destroyed in 1905. In 1907 a reconstructed theatre was opened as *The Playhouse* by Cyril Maude. Comic opera flourished here in the eighties.

The Novelty. Opened in 1882. Rebuilt in 1907, it was named *The Kingsway* (after being known as *The Folies Dramatiques, The Jodrell, The New Queen's, The Eden,* and *The Great Queen Street Theatre*). Its most famous manager was Lena Ashwell.

The Prince of Wales's. Opened in 1884 (originally called *The Prince's*). Farce and musical comedy formed the greater part of its repertoire till it was taken by Forbes Robertson (1898) and Martin Harvey (1900).

Terry's. Opened in 1888 by Edward Terry. Several of Pinero's plays appeared here for the first time.

The Lyric. Opened in 1888 by H. J. Leslie. Musical pieces regularly formed its repertoire until the beginning of the present century.

The Shaftesbury. Opened in 1888 by John Lancaster. Several of Henry Arthur Jones's plays appeared here under the management of E. S. Willard.

The Garrick. Opened in 1889 by John Hare. Many important new plays were given here under Hare's management. Arthur Bourchier took control in 1900.

The Lyric, Hammersmith. Opened in 1890. At first a cheap melodrama house, but brought to distinction by the racy and vital productions of Sir Nigel Playfair.

The Royal English Opera House. Opened in 1891 by R. D'Oyley Carte, later called *The Palace.*

The Duke of York's. Opened in 1892 as *The Trafalgar Square Theatre.* It was renamed *The Duke of York's* in 1895. Here Charles Frohman had his headquarters.

Daly's. Opened in 1893 by Augustus Daly. Famous for its spectacular musical plays. George Edwardes became its manager in 1899.

The Borough, Stratford. Opened in 1896.

The Shakespeare. Opened in 1896.

The Brixton, Lambeth. Opened in 1896 by C. R. Noble.

The Grand, Croydon. Opened in 1896.

The Manor, Hackney. Opened in 1896 by S. A. Went.

The Broadway, New Cross. Opened 1896.

The Grand, Fulham. Opened 1897.

The Alexandra, Stoke Newington. Opened in 1897 by F. W. Purcell.

Her Majesty's. Opened in 1897 by Beerbohm Tree. The scene of Tree's well-known series of Shakespearian revivals. It occupies part of the site covered by the original *Haymarket Theatre* built by Vanbrugh. The name was changed to *His Majesty's* in 1902.

The Princess of Wales's, Kennington. Opened in 1898 by Robert Arthur.

The Coronet, Notting Hill Gate. Opened in 1898.

The Dalston, Hackney. Opened in 1898 by Milton Bode and Edward Compton.

The Crown, Camberwell. Opened in 1898 by Isaac Cohen.

Wyndham's. Opened in 1899 by Charles Wyndham.

The Empress, Lambeth. Opened in 1899 by W. J. Grimes.

The Camden. Opened in 1900 by E. G. Saunders.

The Hippodrome. Opened in 1900.

The Apollo. Opened in 1901 by Henry Lowenfeld. Musical plays formed most of its early repertoire.

The King's, Hammersmith. Opened in 1902.

The New. Opened in 1903 by Sir Charles Wyndham.

The Marlborough, Islington.   Opened in 1903 by F. W. Purcell.

The Scala.   Opened in 1905, on the site of the original *Prince of Wales's*, by Forbes Robertson.

The Aldwych.   Opened in 1905 by Charles Frohman.

The Waldorf.   Opened in 1905, known later as *The Strand*.

The Royal Artillery, Woolwich.   Opened in 1905.

The Globe.   Opened in 1906 as *Hicks' Theatre*.   For some years the London headquarters of Sir Barry Jackson.

The Queen's.   Opened in 1907.

The Playhouse.   Opened in 1907.   See *The Avenue* (1882).

The Kingsway.   Opened in 1907.   See *The Novelty* (1882).

The Little.   Opened in 1910.

The Wimbledon.   Opened in 1910.

The London Opera House.   Opened in 1911.

The Prince's.   Opened in 1911.

The Ambassador's.   Opened in 1913.

Golder's Green.   Opened, as a music hall, in 1913, and as a theatre in 1923.

St. Martin's.   Opened in 1916.

The London Pavilion.   The present house was opened in 1918.   See *The London Pavilion* (1861).

The Winter Garden.   Opened in 1919.

The Everyman, Hampstead.   Opened in 1920.

The New Oxford.   Opened in 1921, on the site of four earlier theatres opened respectively in 1861, 1869, 1873, and 1893.

The Fortune.   Opened in 1924.

The Q.   Opened in 1924.

The Carlton.   Opened in 1927.

The Piccadilly.   Opened in 1928.

The Embassy.   Opened in 1928.

The Dominion.   Opened in 1929.

The Duchess.   Opened in 1929.
Streatham Hill.   Opened in 1929.
The Phœnix.   Opened in 1930.
Prince Edward's.   Opened in 1930.
The Whitehall.   Opened in 1930.
The Cambridge.   Opened in 1930.
The Saville.   Opened in 1931.
The Westminster.   Opened in 1931.

[Besides these theatres, London has had in recent years a number of subscription houses, such as *The Gate* (1925), *The Mercury* (1933), and *The Arts Theatre Club* (1927).   These, although not open to the general public, have had a marked influence upon production methods.]

SUGGESTED READING

The theatre in England possesses a large library, and only a few among the more representative books may here be mentioned. Additional references will be found in specialized volumes dealing with particular periods or aspects of the subject. Especially useful as outlining the pamphlet literature relating to the stage are R. W. Lowe's *A Bibliographical Account of English Theatrical Literature* (1888) ; J. Cameron's *A Bibliography of Scottish Theatrical Literature* (1896 ; in *Transactions of the Edinburgh Bibliographical Society*) ; and J. J. O'Neill's *A Bibliographical Account of Irish Theatrical Literature* (Dublin, 1920). A serviceable list of books is given in Rosamond Gilder's *A Theatre Library* (1932).

Important collections of play bills and other material are to be found at the British Museum, the Victoria and Albert Museum (Mrs. Gabrielle Enthoven collection), and the Widener Library, Harvard (Robert Gould Shaw collection). A " library " of photographic reproductions of illustrative material relating to the stage is being formed at the Department of Drama, Yale University.

GENERAL

R. Farquharson Sharp :
   A Short History of the English Stage, 1909. (Out of print.)
Allardyce Nicoll :
   The Development of the Theatre, 1927.

MEDIÆVAL

E. K. Chambers :
The Mediæval Stage, 1903.
Gustave Cohen :
Histoire de la mise en scène dans le théâtre religieux français du moyen âge, 1926.
Karl Young :
The Drama of the Mediæval Church, 1933.
Alessandro d'Ancona :
Origini del teatro italiano, 1891.
T. C. Peter :
The Old Cornish Drama, 1906.
Allardyce Nicoll :
Masks, Mimes, and Miracles, 1931.

[Useful texts in the volumes issued by The Early English Text Society.]

ELIZABETHAN

E. K. Chambers :
The Elizabethan Stage, 1923.
Crompton Rhodes :
The Stagery of Shakespeare, 1922.
W. J. Lawrence :
The Elizabethan Playhouse, 1912, 1913.
Pre-Restoration Stage Studies, 1927.
The Physical Conditions of the Elizabethan Playhouse, 1927.
J. Q. Adams :
Shakespearean Playhouses, 1917.
A. H. Thorndike :
Shakespeare's Theatre, 1916.
R. Brotanek :
Die englischen Maskenspiele, 1902.

P. Reyher :
   Les masques anglais, 1909.
Enid Welsford :
   The Court Masque, 1928.

[The catalogue of Inigo Jones's designs issued by the Malone and Walpole Societies in 1924 contains many reproductions.]

RESTORATION

Lily B. Campbell :
   Scenes and Machines on the English Stage during the Renaissance, 1923.
R. W. Lowe :
   Thomas Betterton, 1891.
Allardyce Nicoll :
   A History of Restoration Drama, 1923.
Montagu Summers :
   The Restoration Theatre, 1934.
Leslie Hotson :
   The Commonwealth and Restoration Stage, 1928.
Eleanore Boswell :
   The Restoration Court Stage (1660–1702), 1932.

EIGHTEENTH CENTURY

Allardyce Nicoll :
   A History of Early Eighteenth-Century Drama, 1925.
   A History of Late Eighteenth-Century Drama, 1927.
Alwin Thaler :
   Shakespere to Sheridan, 1922.
G. C. D. Odell :
   Shakespeare from Betterton to Irving, 1924.
Colley Cibber :
   An Apology for his Life, 1740.

J. Genest :
> *Some Account of the English Stage,* 1832.

E. A. Parry :
> *Charles Macklin,* 1891.

Thomas Davies :
> *Memoirs of the Life of David Garrick,* 1808.

NINETEENTH CENTURY

Allardyce Nicoll :
> *A History of Early Nineteenth-Century Drama,*
> 1930.

William Hazlitt :
> *A View of the English Stage,* 1821.

Errol Sherson :
> *London's Lost Theatres,* 1926.

Bradlee Watson :
> *Sheridan to Robertson,* 1926.

Thomas Gilliland :
> *The Dramatic Mirror,* 1808.

James Boaden :
> *Memoirs of Mrs. Siddons,* 1827.

H. N. Hillebrand :
> *Edmund Kean,* 1933.

William Archer :
> *William Charles Macready,* 1890.

E. Gordon Craig :
> *The Theatre Advancing,* 1921.
> *Henry Irving,* 1930.

Frank Vernon :
> *The Twentieth-Century Theatre,* 1924.

[*The Theatre,* a journal published from 1879 to 1897, gives a clear picture of late nineteenth-century activities.]

Many books have been published on modern stage endeavour in general, on the work of particular theatres, and on special aspects of theatrical art. Interesting material will also be found in various autobiographies and memoirs. The best journal is *The Theatre Arts Monthly*, which presents a record of the theatre in all countries during recent years. Chiefly concerned with continental activities are H. K. Moderwell's *The Theatre of To-day*, 1914, and K. Macgowan's *Continental Stagecraft*, 1922.

INDEX

THIS index contains all the important subjects, all technical terms, all references to theatres, plays, playwrights, and men and women of the theatre, and most of the references to characters in plays. All theatres are grouped under "Theatre."